Exploring the New Testament

THE FOUR GOSPELS

by Chip Ricks

Virgil W. Hensley, inc.,
Publisher

6116 East 32nd Street • Tulsa, Oklahoma 74135

ISBN 1-56322-039-3

Exploring the New Testament: The Four Gospels

ABOUT THE AUTHOR

Chip Ricks is a professional teacher, workshop leader, conference speaker and lifelong student of the Bible. While teaching at Allan Hancock College, Ricks wrote, and subsequently taught for 12 years, the course from which *Exploring the New Testament* evolved.

In 1984, Ricks left Hancock College to become Director of Adult Ministries at Trinity Church in Lompoc, CA. There the material eventually included in *Exploring the New Testament* was developed and tested in adult classes.

Ricks is the author of several books and has written articles for many religious periodicals.

EXPLORING THE NEW TESTAMENT: THE FOUR GOSPELS

Table of Contents

What *Exploring the New Testament* Is All About VI

Before You Begin, Consider Your Options VII

Lesson 1   The Messiah of the Scriptures *Matthew* 1

Lesson 2   The Beginning of the Gospel *Mark 1-3* 7

Lesson 3   The Secret of the Kingdom *Mark 4:1-34* 15

Lesson 4   The Ministry of Building Faith *Mark 4:35-6:29* 21

Lesson 5   Feeding the Sheep *Mark 6:30-8:21* 27

Lesson 6   The Call to Commitment *Mark 8:22-9:50* 35

Lesson 7   The Journey to the Cross *Mark 10-13* 41

Lesson 8   The Final Sacrifice *Mark 14-16* 47

Lesson 9   The Compassionate, Loving Lord *Luke* 55

Lesson 10   Jesus: The Word of Life *John 1-3* 61

Lesson 11   Jesus: Giver and Sustainer of Life *John 4-7* 69

Lesson 12   Jesus: Light of the World *John 8:1-11:54* 77

Lesson 13   Jesus: The Way, the Truth, and the Life *John 11:55-16:33* .. 83

Lesson 14   Jesus: The Lamb of God *John 17-19* 89

Lesson 15   Jesus: The Resurrected Christ *John 20-21* 95

Appendix 1   The World of the New Testament 101

Appendix 2   The Life of Jesus in the Four Gospels 105

Appendix 3   New Testament Survey 109

Appendix 4   Roman Emperors: The Caesars 111

Map A   Roman Empire in the First Century 113

Map B   Palestine in Jesus' Time 115

Map C   Palestine in Miles 117

Bibliography 119

WHAT EXPLORING THE NEW TESTAMENT IS ALL ABOUT

God's plan has always been to draw us close to Him—to bring us into an intimate relationship simply because He loves us. But many people ignore God because they don't *know* Him. Some people know a lot *about* God, but have not yet come into that close relationship that God desires to have with His children. In the Old Testament, the people were certainly aware of God and His power. They knew it was God who led them out of Egyptian slavery, parted the Red Sea that they might cross, fed them in the wilderness, and led them into the Promised Land. But somehow we have the feeling that only a few of these ancient people ever came to relate to God in a close personal way—the way Moses, Joshua, and David came to know Him.

The four Gospels are the good news that God sent His Son that He might bridge the relationship between us and the Father. *Matthew, Mark, Luke* and *John* tell us about Jesus—who He is, what He came to do, and how He revealed God's plan for us. As you read, you'll get a sense of the everlasting and unchanging love of God. You'll see Jesus, God's Son, revealing Himself step by step to man whom He came to redeem. And you'll see yourself in those who walked with Jesus, struggling with their choices, exercising the free will God gives to us all.

God's Word is a powerful book. It's God speaking to us, and its truths can never be exhausted. But many times we fail to be sensitive to the study of characters, the carefully chosen dialogue, and the deeply embedded themes. Too often, we go right to the interpretation. Historical settings, cultural practices, and varied writing styles dictate our method of study. Being aware of all these factors is important if we are to understand what God is saying to us in His Word.

This study, *The Four Gospels*, will encourage you not only to see the obvious, the literal, but to search beneath the surface, to read with a wider vision, to examine with a critical eye the truths which Jesus often taught through themes and symbols. The focus is always on God's character, man's character, and their relationship. The primary theme, then, is God's relationship to man. But other themes will appear as you move from lesson to lesson. These are the major ideas you should keep in mind as you read.

To give you an overview, *Matthew* and *Luke* have only one lesson each. But, to ensure that you understand God's covenant plan revealed in Christ Jesus and follow the key themes which give it continuity, *Mark* and *John* are studied in greater detail. *Mark* was the first of the four Gospels to be written; *John* was the last. *Mark* is allotted seven lessons, *John* six. Each lesson is divided into several parts allowing you to study at a slower pace and in greater detail if you wish.

Exploring the New Testament: The Four Gospels is designed to stimulate both teachers and students to *hear* what God is saying to us in His Word, to *ask* questions, and to *obey* our God who loves us.

BEFORE YOU BEGIN,
CONSIDER YOUR OPTIONS

This study is planned so that you may learn from God's Word in whatever time you have to spend. Consider your options:

PLAN ONE:

You may choose to read all the way through each Gospel as it is studied. If you are in a class, make notes in the notes column as the lesson is being taught. Later, read the lesson in your notebook and work through the questions under "Exploring." If you aren't in a class, read your lesson first, taking notes as you read. Then, do "Exploring."

The "Search and Decide" questions at the end of each lesson are planned for the advanced Bible student. Finding the answers will take you into both Old and New Testament books in addition to the one in your lesson. You may wish to save "Search and Decide" for future study.

PLAN TWO:

You may choose to move more slowly, reading only the key sections of each book of the Bible being studied. In class, take notes in the notes column provided in your notebook as the lesson is being taught. Then read the lesson in your notebook and answer "Exploring" questions which are most helpful to you.

PLAN THREE:

If you are studying alone rather than with a class, a third option is open to you. Each lesson divides easily into several sections. These sections are indicated by Roman numerals in your lesson. (I, II, III, etc.) Study one or more sections of the lesson as your time permits. As you read, take notes in the notes column provided in your book. Do the reading from your Bible, and answer the "Exploring" questions related to that part of the study. The key to studying alone is consistency in keeping your schedule.

Whatever plan you choose, if you're willing to commit some time to one of the most exciting adventures of your life, you're sure to find a fresh interest and a deeper understanding of God's Word. Most important, you'll come to know Jesus in a closer more intimate way.

When Patrick Henry was near death, he said, "The Bible is worth more than all other books that were ever printed; yet it is my misfortune never to have found time to read it." But, King David, who ruled over a vast kingdom with all its responsibilities, wrote, *"Oh, how I love your law! I meditate on it all day long. . . . My eyes stay open through the watches of the night that I may meditate on your promises"* (Psalm 119:97, 128).

Studies have shown that adults today spend from 40 to 70 hours each week in leisure activities—things they have chosen to do. If our 24-hour day was tithed to the Lord, approximately two and one-half hours daily would be freely given to Him. A choice to spend even a few minutes each day in God's Word is a good beginning.

1

OBEY

HEAR · ASK

THE MESSIAH OF THE SCRIPTURES

READING:
Matthew

OBJECTIVES:
1. You will grasp an overview of the Gospel of Matthew, its distinctive purpose, style and content.
2. You will see Jesus Christ as the fulfillment of God's plan of salvation for man.

THEME:
Jesus Christ, the Messiah

EXPLORING

THE NEW TESTAMENT

For many years the early Church saw no need for a written record of the life and teachings of Jesus Christ, the Messiah. The disciples were there and anxious to teach "all that they had seen and heard." They had been taught by Jesus Himself and were eyewitnesses. And had not Jesus promised to return? They saw no need to plan beyond their generation.

The disciples did write some letters of instruction which were circulated among the churches and later became a part of our Bible, but almost two decades passed before any of the four Gospels was written. Matthew, Mark, and Luke were written between A.D. 50 and 70, but we can't be certain about the precise dates. These three books are called Synoptic Gospels, meaning they're closely related. Scholars tell us that 91% of Mark's Gospel is found in Matthew and 53% is found in Luke. For this reason, many people believe that Mark was the first Gospel to be written. Matthew and Luke do give us many details omitted by Mark, and the three sometimes arrange their material in a slightly different order.

The fourth Gospel was written by John, the beloved disciple of Jesus, sometime between A.D. 85-90—long after the fall of Jerusalem, the death of Peter and Paul, and much suffering of the Christians. For these reasons, it's somewhat different from the other three Gospels.

We will do a close study of Mark and John, but only an overview of Matthew and Luke. Later, you can go back and do a more detailed study of Matthew, which is said to be the most widely read book in the world, and of Luke, which many think has the most beautiful language.

I. THE GOSPEL OF MATTHEW

A. Author

Matthew was a tax collector when he first met Jesus. We suspect that he was much like other tax collectors of his day—hated by Jews who considered him a traitor, and despised by the Romans for his greed. But Jesus loved him. When Jesus called, "Follow me," Matthew left his tax booth and followed to become one of the 12 disciples. As a tax collector he was skilled in writing, a gift which served him well in writing his Gospel.

B. Purpose

Matthew was a Jew writing to Jews. He may not have been convinced that Jesus of Nazareth was the Messiah until after the resurrection. But at that time all doubts were gone. The Gospel which Matthew wrote in later years reflects his deep desire to have his people, the Jews, recognize who Jesus is.

C. Style

Matthew used at least four techniques to accomplish his purpose. First, he began his book with a genealogy running from Abraham, the father of the Hebrew nation, to Jesus Christ. This was the line through whom the prophets said the Messiah would come. Second, Matthew showed Jesus and His ministry as the fulfillment of the Old Testament prophecies. In more than sixty references to Old Testament Scriptures, Matthew pointed out that events which took place were "to fulfill" what was spoken through one of the prophets. Third, Matthew followed the custom of many Jewish writers in using numbers for emphasis. For example, he divided the genealogy at the beginning of the book into three groups of fourteen generations each (three, a divine number; fourteen, twice seven, number of completeness). Fourth, Matthew observed the Jewish reluctance to use God's name. The phrase *"kingdom of heaven"* is unique to this Gospel. Mark and Luke, both Gentile writers, used *"kingdom of God."*

While Matthew did indeed write his Gospel for the Jews, he was also concerned about reaching Gentiles. He closed his book with Jesus' command to *"go therefore and make disciples of all the nations"* (Matthew 28:19).

What was Matthew's purpose in writing his Gospel?

_____

_____

_____

_____

What evidence can you give that this was his purpose?

_____

_____

_____

_____

_____

II. THE MESSIAH OF THE JEWS
(MATTHEW 1:1-28:7)

A. He came. (Matthew 1-4)

God wanted a close relationship with His people. By sending His Son as a little child, God offered us not a relationship of fear but of love.

The birth of the Messiah shouldn't have been a surprise to the Jews. The prophets had foretold that He would be born of a virgin (Isaiah 7:14), that He would be born in Bethlehem (Micah 5:2), and that Magi would come to adore Him (Isaiah 60:3-6). But the Jews envisioned a Messiah who would be a powerful king, one who would reestablish them as a mighty kingdom. When rumors spread, then, that a new king of the Jews had been born, King Herod ordered the slaughter of all infants, thus fulfilling Jeremiah's prophecy (Jeremiah 31:15). Matthew called attention to all these—and more. He didn't forget Isaiah's words that a voice in the wilderness would announce the coming of the Lord (Isaiah 40:3). And he reminds us that Jesus Himself quoted scriptures to fulfill what God had revealed hundreds of years before (Isaiah 9:1-2).

B. He ministered and taught. (Matthew 5-25)

We suspect that Matthew, himself, was a good teacher. He grouped his material around five great lessons which Jesus taught: (1) The Sermon on the Mount (Matt. 5-7); (2) The Commissioning of the Twelve Disciples (Matt. 10); (3) The Kingdom of Heaven (Matt. 13); (4) Teaching the Disciples (Matt. 18); and (5) The Olivet Discourse (Matt. 24-25). Each of these lessons ends with words similar to "when Jesus had ended these sayings."

Matthew began with The Sermon on the Mount and recorded it in Jesus' own words. The sermon began with the Beatitudes—words of comfort and blessing. In this sermon Jesus covered many concerns which are still with us today: murder, revenge, adultery, divorce, prayer, priorities, worry. And He pointed to the loving care of the Father available to all who ask.

During His teaching ministry, Jesus healed the sick, gave sight to the blind and hearing to the deaf. And in doing all these things He fulfilled what was foretold by the prophets.

Take time to see the love of Jesus as He teaches His disciples and all who listen. Think of yourself as one who came to hear Jesus. Listen as He teaches from the Mount of Olives overlooking the city of Jerusalem. Hear what He says as He reveals what is yet to happen at the end of the age.

C. He died and rose again. (Matthew 26:1-28:7)

When Matthew was living through the events surrounding Jesus during Passover week, he didn't understand what was happening. But when he wrote his Gospel, he understood that Jesus fulfilled everything revealed in Scripture about the Messiah.

As Jesus was dying on the cross, He cried out, *"My God, My God, why have You forsaken Me?"* (Matthew 27:46). The words are from Psalm 22:1. Joseph of Arimathea buried Jesus in his own

EXPLORING

THE NEW TESTAMENT

_____

_____

_____

_____

_____

_____

_____

_____

_____

_____

_____

_____

_____

_____

_____

_____

_____

_____

_____

_____

_____

_____

_____

_____

_____

_____

_____

_____

_____

_____

tomb, and a stone was rolled over the door. But Jesus arose on the third day, just as He said He would.

What do you find interesting about the genealogy of Jesus?

_____

_____

_____

_____

_____

As you read through the sermons of Jesus, make a list of five things He said we should do. Put a check by those you find difficult to obey. Pray that God will help you.

_____

_____

_____

_____

III. THE CHOICE AND THE CHALLENGE (MATTHEW 28:8-20)

Although Jesus never spoke about His death without saying He would rise again, no one believed Him. But when the women who came to anoint Jesus' body found the empty tomb and then met Jesus, they *"held Him by the feet and worshiped Him"* (Matthew 28:9) Faced with a choice to believe or not to believe that Jesus had indeed risen from the dead, they believed.

What about the guards? Did they even consider the truth that Jesus was the risen Messiah? We don't know. But we do know that they accepted money from the chief priests to tell a lie.

And what about the disciples? When Jesus first appeared to them, *"they worshiped Him, but some doubted"* (Matthew 28:17). As Jesus stood with the disciples on the mountain in Galilee, He gave them what we know today as The Great Commission—a challenge and a promise. They believed.

All those who heard that Jesus had risen were faced with a choice—to believe or not to believe. And men have faced that choice ever since.

The Gospel of Matthew, written to present Jesus to the Jews as their Messiah, has become a much-loved book by Gentiles as well. To all who read with open hearts, Matthew reveals Jesus as the fulfillment of all the Old Testament prophecies, the One who brought the kingdom of heaven to us.

EXPLORING

What choice faced those who heard that Jesus had risen from the dead? Do we face the same choice today?

_____

_____

_____

_____

What does the challenge Jesus gave the disciples in Matthew 28:18-20 mean to you personally?

_____

_____

_____

_____

EXPLORING

THE NEW TESTAMENT

_____

_____

_____

_____

_____

_____

_____

_____

_____

_____

_____

	THE FOUR GOSPELS			
	MATTHEW	**MARK**	**LUKE**	**JOHN**
DATE	50-70 A.D.	50-70 A.D.	50-70 A.D.	50-70 A.D.
AUTHOR	Matthew Tax Collector Disciple	Mark Young Man	Luke Physician	John Cousin Disciple
AUTHOR'S STYLE	Teacher	Reporter	Historian	Theologian
TO	Jews	Gentiles	Gentiles	World
EMPHASIS	Messiah, Kingship of Jesus	Servanthood of Jesus	Humanity of Jesus	Deity of Jesus
GENEALOGY	Mt. 1:1-17 Abraham— Joseph's Lineage	None	Luke 3:23-38 Adam— Mary's Lineage	None
DISTINCTIVE FEATURES	5 Sermons; Numerous O.T. References; Tightly organized.	Fast Paced; Snapshot pictures; Explained Jewish customs.	Literary; Gentle to women and children.	Doctrinal Symbols

SEARCH AND DECIDE

1. Compare the following scriptures and record the things you learned about the Messiah which were foretold in the Old Testament and fulfilled in Jesus.

Genesis 3:15 and Matthew 1:20 _____

Genesis 22:18 and Matthew 1:1 _____

Jeremiah 23:5 and Matthew 1:1 _____

Isaiah 7:14 and Matthew 1:20-23 _____

Micah 5:2 and Matthew 2:1 _____

Hosea 11:1 and Matthew 2:13-15 _____

Jeremiah 31:15 and Matthew 2:16 _____

Isaiah 11:2 and Matthew 3:16-17 _____

Isaiah 35:5-6 and Matthew 9:35 _____

Psalm 78:1-2 and Matthew 13:34 _____

Zechariah 9:9 and Matthew 21:6-11 _____

Zechariah 11:12 and Matthew 26:15 _____

Isaiah 53:5 and Matthew 27:26 _____

Isaiah 53:12 and Matthew 27:38 _____

Psalm 16:8-10 and Matthew 28:5-6 _____

2. What did you decide about Jesus? Is He the Messiah, the Savior whom God promised to send?

_____

_____

_____

_____

_____

_____

_____

_____

2

HEAR / ASK / OBEY

THE BEGINNING OF THE GOSPEL

READING:
Mark 1-3

OBJECTIVES:
1. You will see that Jesus came with authority over man's body, soul, and spirit.
2. You will understand that the way men respond to Jesus has eternal consequences.

THEMES:
Discipleship
Authority   Kingdom of God
Obedience   Outside/Inside

EXPLORING THE NEW TESTAMENT

Had Mark been born in the 20th century, he might have been editor of a newspaper or perhaps a court reporter. Like any good reporter, he was on the scene when the greatest story ever to be written was being acted out in Palestine. He was a teenager when Jesus began His ministry, and he must have been fascinated by this man from Galilee. We can't be sure how much personal contact he had with Jesus, but Mark was probably the young man hiding behind a tree in the garden when Jesus was arrested. (See Mark 14:51-52.)

We do know that Mark's mother and grandmother were Christians, and that groups of believers often met in their home in Jerusalem. We can imagine that young Mark listened attentively as they talked about Jesus, about the growth of the Church, and about the terrible persecution of believers. Paul took Mark with him on his first missionary journey, but Mark returned to Jerusalem when he discovered Paul's second journey would take him into uncharted, more dangerous territory. Mark was young—perhaps homesick, perhaps just experiencing the concerns of any new Christian who needs time to grow. And he did grow. He accompanied his cousin, Barnabas, on missionary journeys, and later became a close companion of Peter. Shortly before Paul died, Mark visited him in his prison cell in Rome. By this time Mark must have been a mature, strong disciple of Jesus Christ.

Peter, the rough fisherman, had a father-son relationship with Mark. (See I Peter 5:13.) During their many hours together, Peter taught this young follower of Jesus. And during this time, according to an early church father named Papias, Mark wrote down the Apostle's eyewitness account of "all that he remembered of the things said and done by the Lord."

As you read, note the reporter's style in Mark's Gospel. Every word counts, and each action verb is chosen with care. There are few descriptive words and no lengthy interpretations. Mark moves quickly from one scene to another recording what Jesus is teaching through His actions. He raises many questions—but does not always answer them. Mark is concerned with at least one key question important to all of us: What does it mean to be a disciple of Jesus Christ? We find the answer as we see Jesus through Mark's eyes. As you read, try to imagine that you live in the first century A.D. and are hearing about Jesus for the first time.

I. PREPARATIONS ARE MADE (MARK 1:1-15)

A. Preparation for Jesus

Mark began with the *"gospel of Jesus Christ, the Son of God."* Immediately he introduced John the Baptist as the messenger God sent, the *"voice of one crying in the wilderness, 'Prepare the way of the Lord'"* (Mark 1:3).

When John came, the Jews had not heard a prophet's voice in 400 years. The people came from all over the Judean countryside and from Jerusalem to hear him. They came confessing their sins, and John baptized them in the Jordan.

Then John made a startling announcement that One more powerful than he was coming. *"I indeed baptized you with water,"* John said, *"but He will baptize you with the Holy Spirit"* (Mark 1:8).

How were the people being prepared for the coming of the Messiah?

B. Preparation of Jesus

First, Jesus came to be baptized by John. Although He was sinless, His baptism symbolized His willingness to die for us, and foreshadowed His death and resurrection.

Second, to prepare Jesus for His ministry, the Holy Spirit came upon Him *"like a dove."* Then, the Father identified His Son saying, *"You are My beloved Son, in whom I am well pleased"* (Mark 1:11). Mark clearly recognized the work of the Triune God: God the Father, God the Son, and God the Holy Spirit.

Third, Jesus was prepared for His ministry by 40 days in the desert. In the Bible, the wilderness, the sea, and the desert are usually places of testing. And like Moses, Jesus fasted for forty days before beginning His work of bringing to us the New Covenant.

It is characteristic of Mark's writing that he makes the blunt statement, *"John was put in prison,"* (Mark 1:14) but does not at that time tell us why. However, John's work of preparing the way for the coming of the Messiah was finished. And the ministry of Jesus had begun.

So what is the *"Gospel of Jesus Christ, the Son of God"*? What is the good news? The kingdom of God is near!

List those things which prepared Jesus for His ministry.

_____

_____

_____

_____

_____

What *is* the *"Gospel of Jesus Christ"* and the good news of God?

_____

_____

_____

_____

II. JESUS TAKES AUTHORITY (MARK 1:16-2:5)

A. Authority to call men

When Jesus said to Simon and Andrew, *"Come, after me,"* Mark said, *"they left their nets and followed him."* When He called James and John, they left their father, their boat, and their fishing business, and followed Him. (See Mark 1:16-20.) Later, Jesus called Levi, the tax collector: *"Follow me."* And Levi *"arose and followed him"* (Mark 2:14). Although these men were not sure who Jesus was, they recognized His authority to call them to His service.

God looks for men and women who are open and willing to obey Him "at once" when He calls, "Follow me."

B. Authority to teach men

Jesus came announcing that the *"kingdom of God is at hand."* The people were so astonished when they heard Him speak that they talked among themselves and asked, *"What is this? What new doctrine is this?"* (Mark 1:27). They recognized that the teaching of Jesus was different. The difference was the authority with which Jesus taught.

C. Authority to command evil spirits

Mark wanted us to see the authority of Jesus in dealing with the unclean spirit in the man who came to the synagogue at Capernaum. Jesus gave two stern commands: *"Be quiet!"* and *"Come out of him!"* (Mark 1:25). The evil spirit had no choice but to obey.

D. Authority to heal the sick

There is a progression of Jesus' authority in the three stories of healings: Simon Peter's mother-in-law, the leper, and the paralytic. First, Jesus was told Simon's mother-in-law was ill with a fever. Jesus took her hand and the fever left her. He showed His authority over man's body. Next, Jesus met a leper who said, *"If You are willing, You can make me clean"* (Mark 1:40). Jesus was willing to heal not only the man's body but his mind as well. In the third incident, Jesus healed a paralytic and forgave his sins. Jesus demonstrated His authority to heal the whole man—body, soul, and spirit.

In what ways did Jesus show His authority over man's body, mind, and spirit? Give examples.

(1) Body:

(2) Mind:

(3) Spirit:

III. JESUS MEETS CONFLICT
(MARK 2:6-3:12; 3:20-30)

Jesus attracted the attention of the Pharisees. They asked the right questions: "Who can forgive sins but God?" "Why does He eat with tax collectors and sinners?" "How is it that John's disciples and the disciples of the Pharisees are fasting, but yours are not?" "Why are they doing what is unlawful on the Sabbath?" But they really didn't want answers.

The answers Jesus gave the Pharisees were very unconventional. By agreeing that only God could forgive sins, He declared that He was God. In saying that He didn't come to call the righteous, only the sinners, He separated Himself from His accusers. To answer their question about fasting, He gave three illustrations, each showing that His "new doctrine" wouldn't fit into their old molds. And last, Jesus declared that He was Lord of the Sabbath. These teachers of the law were willing to obey the laws of the Sabbath, but were unwilling to obey the Lord of the Sabbath.

Later, when Jesus healed a man with a shriveled hand in the Synagogue on the Sabbath, He posed an interesting question to His accusers: *"Is it lawful on the Sabbath to do good or to do evil, to save life or to kill?"* The teachers were silent, but by their action they answered the question. They *"went out and immediately plotted with the Herodians against Him, how they might destroy Him."* Note that Jesus was angry and *"grieved by the hardness of their hearts"* (Mark 3:4-6). Hardened hearts can separate men from Jesus.

The conflict grew stronger as crowds gathered and Jesus continued to minister. The teachers of the law from Jerusalem accused Jesus of being possessed by Beelzebub. Yet, ironically, whenever the evil spirits saw him, they *"fell down before him and cried out, saying, 'You are the Son of God'"* (Mark 3:11). Jesus pointed out to the "righteous" teachers that their argument did not make sense. He was driving out Satan—and *"If a kingdom is divided against itself, that kingdom cannot stand"* (Mark 3:24). Jesus was fighting a spiritual battle.

In accusing Jesus of being possessed by an evil spirit, the scribes blasphemed against the Holy Spirit. Jesus said this was an eternal sin. He came as the only mediator between God and man. In accusing Jesus of working through Satan's power, the scribes cut off their only means of forgiveness and salvation. Satan cannot forgive sins—or restore us to God. Only God can do this. Rejecting Jesus is a serious sin with eternal consequences.

What was Jesus doing that brought Him into conflict with the leaders of Judaism?

What are some things which can cause us to experience conflict with unbelievers today?

IV. JESUS ESTABLISHES RELATIONSHIPS (MARK 3:13-19, 31-34)

A. Jesus appointed twelve apostles.

Once again Jesus called men to Him—this time the twelve whom He had chosen. Unlike the teachers of the law, they responded obediently to Jesus. He called; they came. Jesus called the 12 to be His disciples for three purposes: (1) to be with Him, (2) to preach, and (3) to heal sicknesses and drive out demons. (See Mark 3:15.) When Jesus calls us to follow Him today, to be His disciples, He calls us for the same purposes. First, we are to spend time with Him. Second, we are to teach others all that we know about our God. And third, we are to enter the spiritual battle against Satan and all his evil.

B. Jesus defined His family.

Jesus wanted the people to see the clear division that was developing between those who were eager to follow Him and those who were rejecting Him.

Note the theme of *outside/inside*. Someone told Jesus that His mother and brothers were outside the house looking for Him. But Jesus' thoughts were on a much larger family—a kingdom family. Some people were standing outside; others were seated around Him in a circle. Those on the outside were asking, looking for Jesus. But He turned to those seated in the circle around him and identified them as His family. Why was this group "inside" His kingdom family? Jesus said it was because they were doing God's will.

These few verses are very important. They answer a key question of Mark's Gospel for us: How do we get into God's family? The crowd was *hearing* and *asking* for Jesus. The circle around Him was *obeying*. To be in God's family, we must *hear*, *ask*, and *obey*.

List the twelve men whom Jesus called to be His disciples.

(1) _____

(2) _____

(3) _____

(4) _____

(5) _____

(6) _____

(7) _____

(8) _____

(9) _____

(10) _____

(11) _____

(12) _____

Give three reasons why Jesus called the twelve disciples.

_____

_____

_____

_____

_____

Jesus came to establish the kingdom of God—His family.
What three things did He say those in His family must do?

_____

_____

_____

_____

_____

_____

Mark plants many questions in our minds—and often we do
not get the answers until later in his Gospel. Make a list of
questions you now have. Then, as you continue in the
Gospel, watch for the answers.

_____

_____

_____

_____

_____

EXPLORING

THE NEW
TESTAMENT

SEARCH AND DECIDE

1. In Mark 2:19-20 Jesus compared Himself to a bridegroom. Read Isaiah 62:5 and John 3:29. What did you learn about the bridegroom? Was John the Baptist content to be the friend of the bridegroom?

_____

_____

_____

_____

_____

_____

_____

_____

2. Read Mark 1:40-45 and Leviticus 13:45-46; 5:2-3. Why do you think Jesus touched the leper? What did you learn from these verses?

_____

_____

_____

_____

_____

_____

_____

_____

_____

_____

3

HEAR / ASK / OBEY

THE SECRET OF THE KINGDOM

READING:
Mark 4:1-34

OBJECTIVES:
1. You will learn the secret of the Kingdom of God.
2. You will be encouraged to seek a greater measure of the Word.

THEMES:
Discipleship   Outside/Inside
Hear/Listen   Kingdom of God

EXPLORING THE NEW TESTAMENT

On November 19, 1863, President Abraham Lincoln delivered an address at the dedication of the national cemetery in Gettysburg, Pennsylvania. The words rang out loud and clear:

"Fourscore and seven years ago, our forefathers brought forth on this continent a new nation, conceived in liberty and dedicated to the proposition that all men are created equal. . . ."

About 15,000 people were present that day to hear Lincoln's words, but as he looked out over the crowd he knew that only a few would remember what he was saying. He scanned the crowd again and said:

"The world will little note nor long remember what we say here; but it can never forget what they did here."

And Lincoln was right. Not many present that day remembered his words. Union soldiers were buried in that cemetery, and some hostile confederate sympathizers were probably in the crowd. A few listeners would drink in every word; some would remember for a short time; others would stop their ears and remember nothing. But with the passage of time, Lincoln's Gettysburg address became one of the best known and most quoted addresses of American history.

Like Lincoln, Jesus faced a crowd which was divided by its reasons for being there. The Pharisees were hostile, and Jesus knew that because of their hard hearts He could not reach them at this time. But those who were open to what He had to say must be taught. Until this time Jesus had publicly declared that He was the Son of God. Now He began to speak in parables, and He began with the Parable of the Sower. Give careful study to this parable. It is the most important one Jesus ever taught. Within it is the secret of the kingdom of God—and the secret of your growth as a Christian.

I. THE PARABLE OF THE SOWER (MARK 4:1-20)

A. The parable

Discipleship for the 12 apostles and for Mark was a process—a movement. And so it is for us. The entire fourth chapter of Mark is important in this process because it is here that Jesus said to those seated around Him, *"To you has been given the secret of the kingdom of God."* This is the first time since chapter one that the *"kingdom of God"* has been mentioned. There Jesus said it was *"at hand"* (Mark 1:15).

Jesus' statement about the secret is in Mark 4:11, immediately following the Parable of the Sower, and all that follows in Chapter 4 explains it! Jesus began the parable with the word "Listen!" He closed with the word "Hear." What lies between those two words is vitally important.

The parable is about a farmer who went out to plant his fields. He scattered the same seed on four different kinds of soil: (1) *"Some seed fell by the wayside."* (2) *"Some fell on stony ground, where it did not have much earth."* (3) *"Some seed fell among thorns."* (4) *"But other seed fell on good ground."* The farmer doesn't change; neither does the seed. Only the soil changes. The difference in the results of the plantings, then, is not the sower and not the seed, but the soil.

Jesus said birds came and ate up the seed which fell by the wayside. The sun scorched and withered the rootless plants which sprang up in the shallow soil of the rocky places. Thorns choked out the seed of the third group. But the fourth group grew, produced, and multiplied—some thirty, some sixty, and some one hundred times.

Then Jesus said, *"He who has ears to hear, let him hea!."* (Mark 4:9).

B. The secret

Some of the people no doubt walked away disappointed that Jesus had told such a simple story. Others probably smiled at their children and were appreciative for such an enjoyable hour. But *"those around Him with the twelve"* were not satisfied. They knew Jesus was teaching a significant truth. They questioned Jesus about the meaning, and received a strange reply:

> *"To you it has been given to know the mystery of the kingdom of God; but to those who are outside, all things come in parables, so that seeing they may see and not perceive, and hearing they may hear and not understand; lest they should turn, and their sins be forgiven them."*
>
> Mark 4:11-12

Once again Jesus divided the people into two groups: those outside and those inside. (See Mark 3:31-35.) Those outside did not have the secret to the kingdom; those inside did. What did those on the inside do that those on the outside did not? If we glance ahead at the interpretation Jesus gave of the Parable of the Sower, we see that all four groups *heard* the word.

But, Jesus taught that once people *hear* the word, they must respond—and not all respond positively. Those who are sincere want to know more; they *ask* for more understanding. And when they understand, they must *obey*. Remember how Jesus identified His family? *"Whoever does the will of God is My brother and My sister and mother"* (Mark 3:35). Quite simply, Jesus said the secret to coming into His kingdom, to being a part of His family, is to *hear* the word, *ask* for more understanding, and *obey* what the word says.

C. The interpretation

Jesus explained that just as seed is sown in four different kinds of soil, so His word is heard by those who respond in different ways.

But the parable is also a picture of our growth as Christians. If we are like those in group one, we hear God's Word when it is read but quickly forget what we have heard. If we are like those in group two, we may hear God speak to us through His Word—but we are not interested enough to ask questions. If we are like those in group three, we are too involved with other things to take time to respond to God's Word when we hear it. Social life, recreational time, even families and church work—all these can choke out God's Word in our lives. The Word is only on the printed page and never becomes a process actively working in our lives. It doesn't produce fruit. It doesn't change us.

But, if we're like those in group four? Well, we're so hungry for the words of Jesus that we *hear* with open ears, *ask* with searching minds, and *obey* with teachable hearts.

Apply Jesus' parable to four groups of people who hear the Word of God today. Give examples.

How might someone in group three move into group four and begin to grow as a Christian?

II. THE LAMP AND THE MEASURE
(MARK 4:21-25)

Jesus compared the Word to light from a lamp and asked, *"Is a lamp brought to be put under a basket or under a bed? Is it not to be set on a lampstand?"* (Mark 4:21). Jesus wanted the people to understand that the kingdom of God was to be like a shining light to the world. What He was teaching about the kingdom was not to be hidden, but put to use.

At this point, Jesus gave the rest of the secret of the kingdom of God. It isn't only the secret of the growth of the kingdom; it's also the secret of our individual growth as Christians. Look at what He said:

> *"Take heed what you hear. With the same measure you use, it will be measured to you; and to you who hear, more will be given."*
>
> Mark 4:24

We might call this "measure for measure." How true this is of God's Word. Jesus said we will be given more understanding only as we use what we have. But He also issued a warning: *"But whoever does not have, even what he has will be taken away from him"* (Mark 4:25).

What evidence do you find in Mark 4:21-25 that God actually does not want the secret which He revealed about the kingdom of God to be kept secret at all?

_____

_____

_____

_____

_____

How does the truth about "measure for measure" apply to your response to God's Word?

_____

_____

_____

_____

_____

III. THE GROWING SEED (MARK 4:26-29)

Jesus said the kingdom of God is like seed planted in the ground. Even when the farmer sleeps the seed sprouts, grows, and produces grain. How does this happen? But then, how does the Word of God suddenly become alive in us? How does it change us? There is a certain mystery about the kingdom of God. We just know that as we *hear*, *ask*, and *obey*, God does His part and His kingdom grows in the hearts of men.

What amazes you most about the growth of the kingdom of God in human hearts?

_____

_____

_____

_____

IV. THE MUSTARD SEED (MARK 4:30-34)

Note how patient Jesus was with those who were trying to understand. He continued to give example after example to those who asked. He gave them the word *"as they were able to hear it"* (Mark 4:33). Jesus said the kingdom of God was like the mustard seed. Yet, this tiny seed can grow to become the largest plant in the garden, so large birds seek shelter in its branches.

It's doubtful that those who heard Jesus could envision His kingdom expanding beyond the Judean borders. But Jesus knew His mission and the future of His kingdom. And for those who would *hear*, *ask*, and *obey*, the kingdom of God was near.

Give an example of a ministry today (hopefully within your church) in which you have seen the kingdom of God grow from a small beginning to great heights.

_____

_____

_____

_____

What evidence do you see in your life that the kingdom of God is like a mustard seed?

_____

_____

_____

_____

SEARCH AND DECIDE

1. Carefully consider these verses:

   Isaiah 5:24 and 6:8-10;
   Ezekiel 2:3-5;
   Mark 4:11-12;
   Hebrews 3:15.

   How important is our response to the Word of God? Does either God or His Word change just because man refuses to listen?

   _____
   _____
   _____
   _____
   _____
   _____
   _____
   _____
   _____
   _____

2. Read the Parable of the Sower in Matthew 13:1-23 and Luke 8:4-15. What additional understanding do you get?

   _____
   _____
   _____
   _____
   _____
   _____
   _____
   _____
   _____

4

HEAR · ASK
OBEY

THE MINISTRY OF BUILDING FAITH

READING:
Mark 4:35-6:29

OBJECTIVES:
1. You will understand Jesus' teaching that fear is the opposite of faith.
2. You will relate to the disciples in their learning process.
3. You will be encouraged to increase your own faith.

THEMES:
Discipleship   Authority
Obedience   Shepherd   Bread
Fear/Faith   Outside/Inside

EXPLORING
THE NEW TESTAMENT

One of the courses required for a teaching credential in most states is practice teaching, generally taught in two semesters. The first semester the student is placed in a classroom with a master teacher—listening, observing, and learning from one who knows the subject well and knows how to teach. The second semester the student finds himself in front of the class putting into practice what he has learned. The master teacher stays close by to encourage and correct—often saving the student from embarrassing situations.

One year a young woman, a student from Cal-Poly University, was placed in an English classroom in a nearby school. She worked hard that year, learning everything she could from her master teacher, a woman known for her excellent teaching. At the end of the year a student in the class said to the new teacher, "You're becoming so much like Mrs. Allison that when I'm listening to you I forget she isn't teaching."

That should be the goal of every Christian: to become so much like Jesus that those who observe us and listen to us and learn from us will see Jesus in us. That must have been young Mark's goal as he wrote his Gospel. It was certainly the goal Jesus had in mind for His disciples. Our focus as we continue in Mark's Gospel is on Jesus, the Master Teacher. The 12 disciples He had chosen were His primary concern, but Jesus taught all who came to Him. He gave special attention to those who asked questions and He encouraged them to obey His words. By all the methods used by good teachers, Jesus built the faith of His students and took away their fear. Let's observe and listen and learn from Him just as the disciples did.

Jesus drew His illustrations and His object lessons from things about Him, and His parables and the things He did often had deeper meaning. Look first to see literally what Jesus said and did. Then look beneath the surface for the lesson He is teaching.

I. THE TEST (MARK 4:35-41)

Some form of the verb "fear" is found over 500 times in our Bible. Sometimes the word means "reverence." This is the kind of fear that we should have for our God. But "fear" is also often the verb meaning "terror." In this sense it's a negative response. Jesus came to bring the kingdom of God to us, and to show us His power over all our fears. He said, "Do not fear." He taught His disciples—and He teaches us—that fear is the opposite of faith.

All day Jesus had been teaching the multitudes from a boat on the Sea of Galilee. Had the disciples understood the Parable of the Sower? Did they understand that He had the power to plant His kingdom in the hearts of men? How great was their faith in this Man of Galilee?

Later, as they were crossing to the other side of the Sea of Galilee, a great storm arose and the disciples became fearful. *"Teacher, do You not care that we are perishing?"* they asked. Jesus ignored the question about His love. He was more concerned about their fear. He rose, rebuked the wind and said to the waves, *"Peace, be still!"* When the sea was calm he asked His disciples, *"Why are you so fearful? How is it that you have no faith?"* (Mark 4:38-40).

At this point the disciples' fear shifted from the sea to Jesus. They were terrified. Who was this Jesus? Never had they seen such power. *"Even the wind and the sea obey him!"* they said. (Mark 4:41).

The disciples responded in the wrong way—in fear rather than in faith. They failed the test. Had we been there, would we, too, have failed?

Why do you think the disciples were so frightened after Jesus calmed the storm?

Recall an experience when you reacted in fear. Share the experience. When did your faith return?

II. THE TEACHING MINISTRY (MARK 5:1-6:6)

A. Jesus healed a demon-possessed man.

They arrived at the other side of the sea, in the region of the Gerasenes. There Jesus drove a legion of demons out of a man who lived in a dark tomb. In ancient Rome a legion consisted of about 6,000 men. This, then, was a serious case of demon possession. But the word of Jesus is powerful. He spoke and the demons were driven into a herd of 2,000 pigs. The herdsmen who witnessed the healing of the man and the destruction of the pigs rushed off to tell the people in the nearby town.

It's important to note how the people and the man who was healed responded to Jesus. The people responded with fear. They *"began to plead with Him to depart from their region"* (Mark 5:17). He honored their request. The man from the tombs, however, reacted quite differently. He didn't fear Jesus. He begged to go with Him. But Jesus had work for the man to do. *"Go home to your friends, and tell them what great things the Lord has done for you, and how he has had compassion on you,"* Jesus said (Mark 5:19). And the man obeyed.

B. Jesus raised a dead girl and healed a woman.

Returning to the other side of the lake, Jesus was met by Jairus, a ruler of the synagogue. Jairus fell at Jesus' feet and pleaded with Jesus to come to his house and heal his dying daughter. Jesus was pleased with the man's faith and started moving through a large crowd to go with him.

In Mark's Gospel, this story of Jairus' daughter is interrupted by an incident which took place on the way to his home. A woman who had been bleeding for 12 years was in the crowd and thought, *"If only I may touch his clothes, I shall be made well"* (Mark 5:28). And she was.

Jesus knew the instant her healing took place, and He sensed her fear. When He asked who had touched Him, the woman *"fearing and trembling . . . came and fell down before Him and told Him the whole truth"* (Mark 5:33). In His compassion, Jesus took away her fear and gave her His peace.

As Jesus was talking with the woman, a messenger arrived with the news that Jairus' daughter was dead. But Jesus ignored the message and said to the ruler of the synagogue, *"Do not be afraid; only believe"* (Mark 5:36). When they arrived at Jairus' house, Jesus took Peter, James, and John, along with the child's parents, into the room where the little girl lay. Those waiting outside missed the miracle which took place inside the room because they had no faith in Jesus' power to raise the child from death.

C. Jesus taught in Nazareth.

Jesus and His disciples went on to Nazareth, Jesus' hometown, and there Jesus taught in the synagogue. Those who heard Him were amazed at His wisdom, yet was He not Mary's son, the village carpenter? Their unbelief hindered the work of the kingdom. Jesus was saddened that His close friends did not believe Him. *"He marveled because of their unbelief"* (Mark 6:6).

EXPLORING

THE NEW TESTAMENT

Explain the results of fear as you find them in the stories of the demoniac, Jairus' daughter, and the people of Nazareth.

Fear of death is common to most people. When Jairus' daughter was near death, Jesus said to him, *"Do not be afraid; only believe."* In what way are these words helpful to you?

III. THE SECOND TEST (MARK 6:7-13)

Were the disciples ready for another test? They had watched as Jesus cast demons out of a man, as He healed a woman who touched His clothes, as He raised a little child from death to life. They had observed the results of having faith in Jesus—and they knew that fear could hinder the work of His ministry. They had *heard*; they had *asked* questions; would they *obey*?

Remember, Jesus called the disciples for a three-fold purpose: to be with Him, to go out to preach, and to have authority to heal sicknesses and to cast out demons (See Mark 3:15.) They had been with Jesus for some time. Now He sent them out *"two by two and gave them power over unclean spirits"* (Mark 6:7).

With what faith they had, the disciples *"preached," "cast out many demons,"* and *"anointed with oil many who were sick, and healed them"* (Mark 6:12-13). Their faith was growing.

Why do you think Jesus gave the disciples such specific instructions before He sent them out to minister?

Recall a time when you knew Jesus was asking you to do a difficult task. How did you react? Was your faith tested?

_____

_____

_____

_____

IV. THE INTERLUDE (MARK 6:14-29)

Why did Mark break into his Gospel at this point with a more detailed story of John the Baptist? We were told earlier only that he was in prison. Perhaps Mark wanted us to see the ongoing plan for the kingdom: John's work was finished, and the disciples' work was beginning.

Herod Antipas feared the truth that John the Baptist preached and put him in prison. Later he feared the reaction of his dinner guests and of his wife, Herodius, if he broke the rash vow he had made. His fear triumphed, and he had John beheaded. Within a few short years Herod Antipas would be faced with another decision: Jesus would be brought before him for trial.

Jesus saw fear as an enemy—the opposite of faith. As He said to Jairus, He says to us, _"Do not be afraid; only believe."_

What did Herod Antipas fear which caused him to make bad choices?

_____

_____

_____

_____

What are some of the fears we might have today which can result in hindering God's work?

_____

_____

_____

_____

Briefly relate a time when God took away fear and gave you peace.

_____

_____

_____

_____

SEARCH AND DECIDE

1. The word translated "fear" from the Hebrew is sometimes "yare" meaning "reverence." List three things you learn about "fear" from the following verses.

   Exodus 1:17, 20, 21; 20:20
   Psalm 2:11; 34:4, 9
   Proverbs 14:2

   _____

   _____

   _____

   _____

   _____

   _____

   _____

   _____

2. We can understand why Jesus wouldn't allow evil spirits to announce who He was, but why did He command people not to tell? Reread the following instances we have seen so far in Mark, and one in Matthew that Mark doesn't record, and then decide.

   Mark 1:40-45; 5:18-20, 40-43
   Matthew 9:27-31

   _____

   _____

   _____

   _____

   _____

   _____

   _____

   _____

5

HEAR ASK OBEY

FEEDING THE SHEEP

READING:
Mark 6:30-8:21

OBJECTIVES:
1. You will identify with the disciples in their learning process.
2. You will want to become the kind of shepherd Jesus wants you to be.

THEMES:
Discipleship
Bread
Shepherd

EXPLORING THE NEW TESTAMENT

God must have a special love for shepherds. Abraham, Isaac, and Jacob were shepherds. Moses left his position in Pharaoh's palace to become a shepherd in the desert for forty years. David was called to leave his flock of sheep and to become king of Israel. The patriarchs, Moses, and David all learned to shepherd God's people by first caring for sheep. And each learned to obey and follow the leading of the Good Shepherd. Isaiah the prophet wrote of the Lead Shepherd:

> "He will feed His flock like a shepherd; He will gather the lambs with His arm, And carry them in His bosom, And gently lead those who are with young."
>
> Isaiah 40:11

God has always intended that those who lead His people and teach them should care for them as a gentle, compassionate shepherd who puts the needs of his sheep above his own. But the prophet Ezekiel said that in his day the shepherds of Israel were feeding themselves and neglecting their people. God said He would hold these shepherds accountable. Zechariah also dealt with worthless shepherds in his day and warned that the shepherd who did not care for his flock would be judged. The world was in great need of good shepherds.

When Jesus was born, the angels announced His coming first to the shepherds in the fields *"keeping watch over their flock by nigh."* (Luke 2:8).

Perhaps this is significant because Jesus' plan was to teach and train His disciples to watch over His people—to feed and care for them as good and faithful shepherds.

Watch Jesus closely as He teaches His disciples that they are to feed His sheep. As His followers today, we are called to the same task.

I. FEEDING THE FIVE THOUSAND (MARK 6:30-44)

The twelve disciples were tired when they returned to Jesus after their first missionary trip. Often weary Himself,

Jesus understood, and suggested that they cross the lake to a quiet place and rest. But drawing near to shore, they saw a huge crowd waiting. Jesus *"was moved with compassion for them, because they were like sheep not having a shepherd."* And He began to teach them. But the disciples, tired and hungry, asked Jesus to *"send them away"* (Mark 6:34-36). When Jesus suggested that instead they feed the crowd, the disciples didn't understand. Then, the Master Teacher sent His disciples in search of food, and they returned with five loaves and two fish.

Patiently Jesus directed them to seat the people in groups. Then He took the loaves and fish, gave thanks, and gave the food to His disciples to distribute to His sheep. The people ate and were satisfied. Afterwards the disciples picked up twelve basketsful of broken pieces of bread and fish.

What did Jesus want the disciples to learn? What does He want us to learn? These 5,000 people were on their way to Jerusalem for the Passover Feast. Surely this feast was on Jesus' mind that day. As He fed the 5,000, He foreshadowed another Passover Feast when He would relinquish His place as the Shepherd to become the Lamb. If the disciples could not learn that He was their spiritual food, who would shepherd His sheep?

How often do we miss the lessons Jesus wants to teach us through the daily experiences of our lives? When we are tired, frustrated, focused on our physical needs, we can easily fail to recognize what Jesus would have us do.

EXPLORING

What evidence do you find that the crowd was ready to be fed? What was Jesus' attitude toward their need? What about the disciples' attitude?

Recall a time when you were very tired, yet were called upon to minister to someone. What was your attitude? What can you learn from the lesson Jesus taught?

II. UNDERSTANDING ABOUT THE LOAVES (MARK 6:45-56)

Jesus sent the disciples ahead of him to Bethsaida, and he went up on the mountainside to pray. Later that evening, Jesus walked out on the water and meant to pass the disciples by, but they saw Him and cried out in terror. Jesus spoke to them immediately saying, *"Be of good cheer! It is I; do not be afraid"* (Mark 6:50). Then He got into the boat, and the sea was calm.

The disciples were no longer afraid, but Mark tells us that they were *"greatly amazed."* Why? Were they amazed because Jesus calmed the sea? Or because He walked on water? They had observed His power over the sea on at least one other occasion. If He could calm the winds, could He not walk on water? No, the root of their reaction, Mark said, was that *"they had not understood about the loaves because their heart was hardened"* (Mark 6:52)

The disciples were much like many people today. God's miracles are all around us, but there are those who work hard to explain them as "coincidence" or "chance" or "fate." The disciples watched all the miracles, saw the power of Jesus, but they did not believe that He was indeed the Christ. They did not understand about the bread.

It is also difficult for us to get where Jesus wants us to go if we are not moving in the right direction. Jesus had sent the disciples to Bethsaida, but they landed in Gennesaret. Like all of us, they still had much to learn.

What did Mark mean when he said the disciples' amazement at seeing Jesus walk on water was due to their lack of understanding about the loaves?

III. FACING THE PHARISEES (MARK 7:1-23)

The Pharisees heard that Jesus had been in the marketplace—a place they considered defiled. But there Jesus had touched many sick people and made them well. Later these Pharisees caught the disciples eating with unclean hands and accused Jesus of allowing His disciples to break the tradition of the elders. This offered an opportunity for Jesus to teach His disciples and everyone who would listen that things on the "outside" don't make a man unclean. Only those things on the "inside" of man corrupt him. This should cause us to question our motives for the things we do.

What "outside" things were the Pharisees doing which set aside the commands of God? Why were their actions meaningless?

What did Jesus name as some of the "inside" things which corrupt?

IV. RECEIVING EVEN THE CRUMBS (MARK 7:24-30)

To teach His disciples privately, Jesus left Galilee and went up to Tyre, a Gentile city. There a Syrophoenician woman heard about Him and came begging Him to drive an evil spirit out of her little daughter. Because the disciples had not learned about the "bread," this was another opportunity for a lesson. Jesus told the woman it was not right to *take the children's bread and throw it to the little dogs* (Mark 7:27). Strangely enough, the woman understood more than the disciples! And she was not afraid.

The Jews called Gentiles "dogs." This Gentile woman was willing to acknowledge that Jesus had come first to the Jew— then to her people. She accepted the crumbs. She wanted them. Are we that hungry for Jesus? Jesus was well pleased with this woman and honored her request.

Jesus was well pleased with the attitude of the Syrophoenician woman. Why?

V. OPENING THE EARS AND MOUTH
(MARK 7:31-37)

Jesus yearned to open the ears of His disciples that they might *hear* what He was saying and *speak* His words to others. In Decapolis, another opportunity came for an object lesson.

A man who could neither hear nor speak was brought to Jesus for healing. Jesus took him away from the crowd, perhaps that He might better teach His disciples. He put His fingers in the man's ears, and then spit and touched the man's tongue. Looking up to heaven, Jesus said, *"Be opened!"* And the man heard and spoke. Did the disciples understand the lesson?

Jesus healed the man's hearing before He touched his tongue and healed his speech. What might this teach us?

_____

_____

_____

_____

VI. FEEDING THE FOUR THOUSAND
(MARK 8:1-13)

Still in the Decapolis, Jesus had been feeding a crowd of 4,000 people spiritual food for three days. They had not asked for any other bread, but Jesus had compassion on them and suggested to the disciples that they should be fed. But where was the bread to come from? Where indeed! Jesus repeated the lesson and fed the 4,000.

Why do you think Jesus found it necessary to repeat the lesson He taught the disciples when He first fed 5,000 people?

_____

_____

_____

_____

VII. WARNING ABOUT THE LEAVEN
(MARK 8:14-21)

As they crossed to the other side of the lake, Jesus' thoughts were still on His lesson about the bread. He warned

_____

_____

_____

_____

_____

_____

_____

_____

_____

_____

_____

_____

_____

_____

_____

_____

_____

_____

_____

_____

_____

_____

_____

_____

_____

_____

_____

_____

_____

_____

His disciples, *"Take heed, beware of the leaven of the Pharisees and the leaven of Herod"* (Mark 8:15). Mark tells us that they had forgotten to bring bread—except for one loaf they had with them in the boat. Even then, they said, *"We have no bread"* (Mark 8:16).

How desperately Jesus wanted them to understand His teaching and His mission. But their thoughts were so much on the material that they could not see the spiritual. With questions and answers Jesus repeated the lesson on bread.

What is there in our society today which might be considered *"leaven of the Pharisees?"*

_____

_____

_____

_____

_____

SEARCH AND DECIDE

1. Read Genesis 12:3 and Galatians 3:6-9. What evidence did you find in this lesson that these scriptures were being fulfilled?

_____

_____

_____

_____

_____

_____

_____

_____

2. Look again at Mark 6:30-8:21 and focus on Jesus as the model Teacher and Shepherd. Make a list of what you can apply as you teach and shepherd those entrusted to your care.

_____

_____

_____

_____

_____

_____

_____

_____

6

HEAR · ASK · OBEY

THE CALL TO COMMITMENT

READING:
Mark 8:22-9:50

OBJECTIVES:
1. You will understand that Christ's call to follow Him means to suffer, be rejected, die, and rise.
2. You will be challenged to evaluate your own commitment as a disciple of Jesus Christ.

THEMES:
Discipleship
Suffer, Be Rejected, Die, Rise

EXPLORING THE NEW TESTAMENT

I n 1982, Irina Ratushinskaya was sentenced to seven years of hard labor and five more years of internal exile in Soviet Russia for writing poetry about Christian faith and human rights. She was released after four years of intense suffering from the cold, near starvation, and torture, because of the prayers and public outcry of Christian groups in the West.

In her book, *Grey Is the Color of Hope*, Irina Ratushinskaya tells her story—a story of courage, faith, and ministry to other prisoners. She refused to allow herself to become bitter toward her captors realizing that if they could bring her to hate them, they would win. Instead, she was sustained by the love of God and the sense of His presence with her.

Irina is only one of millions of believers who have suffered for the cause of Jesus Christ. Like the first century Christians, these believers came to understand that the call to commitment which Jesus gave was not a call to easy living. It was a call to follow in His steps—and His steps led to the cross.

Some theologians today believe that we have weakened the call of Christ in our century; indeed, many people seek to follow a messiah of their own making. The disciples, too, had a different picture of the Messiah until Jesus met them at a crossroads and called them to commit themselves to a Savior born to die. Listen carefully to the words of Jesus in this lesson. He speaks with authority.

I. THE SECOND TOUCH (MARK 8:22-9:1)

A. For the blind man

In Bethsaida, some people brought a blind man to Jesus and begged Him to touch him. The touch of Jesus had healed Peter's mother-in-law, a leper, Jairus' daughter, many others. But total healing for this blind man would come only from a second touch, and this had not happened before. Why now? Was Jesus teaching a lesson that His disciples must learn?

Jesus led the blind man away from the crowd, put spittle on the man's eyes, and touched them with His hands. Then Jesus asked him if he saw anything. The man must have been facing Jesus, yet he replied, *"I see men like trees, walking"* (Mark 8:24).

Once more Jesus put his hands on the man's eyes. This time *"he was restored and saw everyone clearly"* (Mark 8:25).

B. For the disciples

Did the disciples understand that, like the blind man, they were not seeing Jesus clearly? Did they not know how much He wanted to open their eyes if only they would focus on Him? It is strange that the disciples did not question Jesus about this unique healing of the blind man.

They went on to Caesarea Philippi, a city of many pagan gods. Jesus had started down the long road that would lead Him to Jerusalem and His death. If the disciples wanted Him to be their God, then all other gods must go. As they approached the city, Jesus asked His disciples, *"Who do men say that I am?"* The disciples knew the answer to this question—John the Baptist, Elijah, one of the prophets. Then Jesus asked the much more important question: *"But who do you say that I am?"* (Mark 8:29). And Peter answered, *"You are the Christ"* (Mark 8:29).

The disciples had come to the fork in the road. When they acknowledged Jesus as the Messiah, His teaching changed. Now He spoke plainly, not in parables. He told them that He must suffer many things, be rejected, be killed, and after three days rise again. But Peter could not accept this new revelation from the Christ. Jesus immediately recognized that Satan had his hand on Peter and commanded, *"Get behind Me, Satan!"* (Mark 8:33). When Jesus gave Satan this command, He may have been reminding Peter to follow Him.

Then Jesus called the crowd and His disciples to Him, and taught them the hard truth about discipleship. *"Whoever desires to come after Me,"* He said, *"let him deny himself, and take up his cross, and follow Me"* (Mark 8:34).

What lesson do you think Jesus wanted the disciples to learn as they watched Him heal the blind man?

_____

_____

_____

_____

_____

II. THE CONFIRMATION (MARK 9:2-13)

Six days passed, and then Jesus took three of His disciples—Peter, James and John—with Him for special teaching. On top of a mountain the disciples saw Jesus in all His power. He was transfigured before them, his clothes dazzling white. Then two others appeared: Elijah and Moses. The experience was overwhelming for the three disciples. Only Peter could speak. Looking at Jesus he blurted out, *"Let us make three tabernacles:*

one for You, one for Moses, and one for Elijah" (Mark 9:5). Peter placed Jesus on the same level with Moses and Elijah, and Moses and Elijah are not God. Jesus is.

At once a voice said, *"This is my beloved Son. Hear him!"* (Mark 9:7). Peter was corrected. God set Jesus apart. Elijah and Moses disappeared and the disciples saw only Jesus.

What was the purpose of this experience which we call the transfiguration? First, it was a confirmation for Peter, James and John. Jesus was entrusting the kingdom of God to them. They must not fail. Second, it was a confirmation for Jesus Himself. God confirmed His Son and His mission again.

As they went down the mountain, Jesus told His three disciples not to tell anyone what they had seen until He rose from the dead. And they obeyed.

What evidence do you find that this experience had an impact on the three disciples?

_____

_____

_____

_____

Recall a time when you had a mountaintop experience with God. In what way was your faith in Him confirmed?

_____

_____

_____

_____

III. THE STRONG TEACHING (MARK 9:14-50)

A. Why do we fail?

Jesus was on His way to the cross. Could He trust the disciples with His mission to the world? At the foot of the mountain they saw a great crowd and heard scribes ridiculing the disciples. A man had brought his son, possessed of an evil spirit, to the disciples and they could not drive out the spirit. *"They could not."* These words must have cut into Jesus' heart.

Jesus commanded the spirit to leave the boy and it did. All power rests in Jesus. Nothing is impossible with Him. Why, then, do we so often fail? Is it that we forget the source of our power and try to act on our own?

B. Won't you believe?

Jesus left the crowds because He was teaching His disciples. *"The Son of Man is being delivered into the hands of men,"* He said.

"*They will kill him. And after He is killed, He will rise the third da.*" (Mark 9:31). The disciples didn't understand, and they were "*afraid to ask.*" In our walk with Christ aren't we at times like the disciples—afraid to ask because we fear the truth of what it means to follow Jesus?

C. Who is greatest?

Not only did the disciples not ask questions, they erased from their minds all that Jesus had been saying to them. They wanted their Messiah to rule the earth, on the earth, in a great kingdom. As they walked, they argued among themselves about who was the greatest. Jesus stopped and called the disciples to Him. "*If anyone desires to be first,*" He said, "*he shall be the last of all, and servant of all*" (Mark 9:35).

D. Who is for us?

The power struggle in the hearts of the disciples was still going on when they saw a man casting out demons in Jesus' name. Was this man taking upon himself authority reserved for the twelve disciples of Jesus? The disciples ordered the man to stop, "*because he does not follow us*" (Mark 9:38). But note what Jesus said: "*Do not forbid him. . . . For he who is not against us is on our side*" (Mark 9:39-40). We need to learn this lesson today.

E. Why the warning?

The lesson wasn't complete. Jesus continued by cautioning the disciples against causing "*little ones who believe in Me to stumble*" (Mark 9:42). The man who was casting out demons in Jesus' name was just beginning his journey to understanding. The disciples had been with Jesus a long time. Didn't rank have its privileges? No, Jesus said. Not in His kingdom.

Jesus' way for the disciples, and for us, is the way of servanthood. "*Have salt in yourselves, and have peace with one another,*" Jesus said (Mark 9:50). Salt is the flavoring and the preserving agent in meat. The disciples were in the midst of a dying and corrupt society. They had a common task, and would be brought together in their suffering as a preserving agent for mankind. Our society is still dying and corrupt. And Christians are still called to stand together and be salt in our world.

We may never have to suffer like Irina Ratushinskaya, but Christ's call "*Follow me*" is still a call to suffer, be rejected, die, and rise with Him.

Why were the disciples unable to drive out the evil spirit? Why do we sometimes fail to accomplish what Jesus has asked us to do?

Why did the disciples find it hard to accept a Messiah who was to suffer, be rejected, die and rise? Why do people today find this hard?

_____

_____

_____

_____

_____

EXPLORING

THE NEW
TESTAMENT

_____

_____

_____

_____

_____

_____

_____

_____

_____

_____

_____

_____

_____

_____

_____

_____

_____

_____

_____

_____

_____

_____

_____

_____

_____

_____

_____

SEARCH AND DECIDE

1. Read Matthew 4:8-10 and compare with Mark 8:31-33. In what way was Jesus' temptation like that of Peter? Does Satan still use this temptation today?

_____

_____

_____

_____

_____

_____

_____

_____

2. See what additional information you can gather about the appearance of Moses and Elijah on the mountaintop with Jesus by reading Malachi 4:5-6, Luke 9:31, and Luke 24:27. Why would this experience be an encouragement to Peter, James and John?

_____

_____

_____

_____

_____

_____

_____

_____

7

HEAR · ASK · OBEY

THE JOURNEY TO THE CROSS

READING:
Mark 10-13

OBJECTIVES:
1. You will become aware of those things Jesus thought most important as He taught and ministered on the way to the cross.
2. You will see the authority of Jesus over religious institutions, governments, life, the law, people.
3. You will understand the warnings of Jesus about the future.

THEMES:
Authority   Inside/Outside
Suffer, Be Rejected, Die, Rise

Jesus began the long journey to Jerusalem knowing that there He would suffer death on the cross. Rejection had already begun. Many Galileans who had looked to Him as the one who would be their earthly king were disappointed when they learned that His kingdom was *"not of this world."* When Jesus taught that if anyone wanted to be His disciple, he must *"deny himself, and take up his cross, and follow Me,"* few were willing (Mark 8:34). The journey with His disciples from Capernaum took Him across the mountains of Samaria, south into Judea, then across the Jordan into Perea before He reached Jerusalem.

As we might expect, the ministry of Jesus—His teaching and His healing—became more intense. There was little time left, and everywhere He looked He saw *"sheep without a shepherd."* He must have felt discouraged that no one understood the Father's plan. Even the disciples continued to seek personal glory in an earthly kingdom. Twice Jesus had told them plainly that He must suffer, be rejected, die, and rise again, but they could not understand such hard teaching.

As you walk with Jesus on His journey to Jerusalem, listen carefully to His teaching. He speaks with authority. See Him enter Jerusalem as the Servant-King. Heed His warnings about the future.

EXPLORING THE NEW TESTAMENT

I. JESUS TAUGHT AND MINISTERED ON THE WAY TO THE CROSS (MARK 10)

A. He taught the Pharisees.

The Pharisees came to Jesus with the question, *"Is it lawful for a man to divorce his wife?"* Jesus focused on God's original intention, His ideal for man and woman. At creation, Jesus said, God *"made them male and female"* that the two might become *"one flesh."* But, *"because of the hardness of your heart,"* Jesus said, *"he [Moses] wrote you this precept"* (Mark 10:2-8).

Jesus established equality between men and women when He suggested that men as well as women should be held accountable for committing adultery. This was a new teaching to the Jews of this time.

B. He ministered to the children.

Perhaps Jesus was thinking of broken homes caused by divorce when he said to the disciples, *"Let the little children come to Me, and do not forbid them; for of such is the kingdom of God"* (Mark 10:14). To enter the kingdom, hearts must not be hard, but rather as tender as a child's.

C. He taught a rich young man.

As they continued their journey, a rich young man came and knelt humbly before Jesus, asking, *"Good Teacher, what shall I do that I may inherit eternal life?"* (Mark 10:17). But, like many people today, he came to Jesus as the "Good Teacher" and did not accept Him as the Messiah, the Son of God. Jesus told him to give to the poor that he might become servant of all and fulfill the requirements of being first in the kingdom. The Law and the commandments the man knew so well could not make him "good" or "first"; they could only point him toward God. The man made his choice and went away from Jesus sad.

D. He taught the disciples.

Once again on the road to Jerusalem, Jesus took the Twelve aside. He explained His mission for the third time. In Jerusalem, He told them, He would be "delivered" to the chief priests and scribes, "condemned to death," "mocked," "scourged," "spit on," and "killed." Three days later He would "rise."

But the disciples held tightly to the Christ of glory and could not accept Isaiah's Suffering Servant. (See Isaiah 53.) James and John came to Jesus asking to sit on His right and left when He came into His glory. But Jesus said, *"Whoever of you desires to be first shall be slave of all"* (Mark 10:44).

E. He ministered to blind Bartimaeus.

The eyes of the disciples were still seeing only dimly when a blind beggar cried out, *"Jesus, Son of David, have mercy on me!"* He knew who Jesus was! James and John had asked for glory; blind Bartimaeus asked for sight. Jesus healed him and he *"followed Jesus on the road"* (Mark 10:47, 52).

Compare the attitudes of the Pharisees and the rich man as they came to Jesus with questions.

What qualities of little children must we have when we come to Jesus?

II. JESUS ENTERED JERUSALEM AS A KING (MARK 11:1-26)

When the King of kings entered Jerusalem on that first day of Passover week, He rode on a borrowed colt. (See Zechariah 9:9.) His escort was a crowd of poor people who spread before Him their garments and some branches they had cut in the fields. They were a joyful group, shouting "Hosanna!" and singing. Ironically, however, within a few hours, many in the crowd would join the Pharisees and Sadducees, now lurking in the background, in a determined effort to kill this One who claimed to be the Messiah.

Late in the day, Jesus went to the Temple, looked around, and left with His twelve disciples for Bethany, a few miles away.

But Jesus returned to Jerusalem the next morning as a judge. He began with a fig tree which had no fruit, condemning it to remain forever fruitless. Next, He cast the moneychangers and businessmen out of the Temple. By these actions Jesus acted out a parable of Israel. The fig tree is a time-honored symbol of Israel, but like the fig tree, Israel had produced no fruit. There were no Gentiles in the Temple, and God's house of prayer had been turned into a place of business. Both the nation of Israel and the Temple were judged.

The next morning as Jesus and His disciples again passed by the withered fig tree, Jesus taught them that the prayer of faith can accomplish the impossible. But, such prayers must come from forgiving hearts.

What expectations for Jesus and His kingdom did the disciples have?

_____

_____

_____

_____

Why did Jesus judge the fig tree, the Temple, and the nation of Israel? Do you think we will be judged for the same thing?

_____

_____

_____

_____

III. JESUS HAS ALL AUTHORITY (MARK 11:27-12:44)

In 1989 the world watched in amazement as many men who had once had great authority and control over millions of people in communist countries tumbled from power. All of them fought to retain their positions. In first century

THE NEW TESTAMENT

Jerusalem, the Jews feared a similar fall. Although often separated by their own internal battles for power, the Pharisees and Sadducees joined together to test the authority of Jesus and expose Him to the crowds.

First, Jesus established His authority over religious institutions. When the leaders of Judaism questioned His authority to cleanse the Temple, Jesus answered them with a parable about a man who planted a vineyard and left it in the care of tenants who failed to produce a harvest. The religious leaders understood that Jesus was condemning them because they had not only failed to produce fruit, but had mistreated and killed the prophets. Through the parable, Jesus revealed their plan for killing Him and declared that the owner of the vineyard would give it to other more responsible tenants.

Next Jesus established His authority over governments. The Pharisees joined with the Herodians, normally their enemies, to test Jesus. They asked, *"Is it lawful to pay taxes to Caesar or not? Shall we pay, or shall we not pay?"* (Mark 12:14-15). Jesus called for a coin bearing Caesar's inscription and said, *"Render to Caesar the things that are Caesar's, and to God the things that are God's"* (Mark 12:17). This answer which amazed all who heard established the principles separating church and state by which we live today.

Third, Jesus declared His authority over life in a conversation with the Sadducees as they tried to trap Him. This powerful group denied life after death, yet their question concerned marriage at the resurrection. Jesus gave them an answer which confirmed life after death and closed the conversation by saying, *"You are therefore greatly mistaken"* (Mark 12:27).

Fourth, Jesus declared His authority over the Law by answering a scribe who asked which commandment was the most important. Jesus quoted from Deuteronomy 6:4–5. *"Love the Lord your God with all your heart, with all your soul, with all your mind, and with all your strength."* Then He added, *"You shall love your neighbor as yourself"* (Mark 12:30-31)

And last, Jesus declared His authority over people. He pointed to the Scriptures and to Himself not as David's son, but as David's Lord. Then, as Lord, Jesus sat down to watch the crowd putting their money into the Temple treasury. By this action He established His authority to judge people's hearts.

Briefly explain what Jesus meant by the parable of the tenants. Does this parable have anything to say to people today?

Over what areas did Jesus clearly establish His authority?

_____

_____

_____

_____

_____

IV. JESUS KNOWS THE FUTURE (MARK 13)

Jesus and the disciples left the Temple and went to the Mount of Olives where Jesus sat down opposite the Temple. There He prophesied that the Temple would be totally destroyed. When the disciples asked Him when this would happen, He commanded them to *"take heed,"* to *"watch."* Most authorities believe that part of the prophecy was fulfilled at the time the Temple was destroyed in A.D. 70. But there is more and the warnings are still applicable to us today as we await the total fulfillment of the prophecy on the final Day of the Lord. Briefly the four warnings are: (1) Watch out for false christs who will lead many astray. (2) Watch out for yourselves because of persecutions which are sure to come. (3) Watch for changes and social chaos throughout the world. (4) Watch lest you be found sleeping because no one knows the day or the hour when Jesus will return.

As Christians, we are not to be concerned about the dates when God will bring all these things to pass. Rather, Jesus gave these prophecies that we might be more watchful in our daily walk and know that we are secure in Him.

What are some of the things Jesus said would happen before He returns?

_____

_____

_____

_____

_____

What did Jesus say our attitude about the future should be? Is this your attitude?

_____

_____

_____

_____

_____

SEARCH AND DECIDE

1. Read Luke 13:6-9. Some scholars believe that Jesus told this parable a short time before the incidents Mark records in Mark 11:12-14; 20-25. How does the parable help you understand Mark's report?

_____

_____

_____

_____

_____

_____

_____

2. Peter was present when Jesus taught about the future. (See Mark 13.) Later he wrote about the events yet to come in II Peter 3:3-17. What did Peter learn from Jesus that is helpful to you?

_____

_____

_____

_____

_____

_____

_____

_____

8

HEAR / ASK / OBEY

THE FINAL SACRIFICE

READING:
Mark 14-16

OBJECTIVES:
1. You will understand how the symbols of the Old Covenant led God's people to the New Covenant in Christ Jesus.
2. You will relate to the disciples in their weakness.
3. You will see Jesus as the final sacrifice and the hope of mankind.

THEMES:

Covenant	Numbers	Sacrifice
Obedience	Passover	
Suffer, Be Rejected, Die, Rise		

EXPLORING THE NEW TESTAMENT

George Frederick Handel was composing music at the age of eleven. But at the height of his career, in 1737, he had a stroke which left him partially paralyzed. Many thought Handel's musical career was ended, yet in the depths of despair he wrote his greatest work, *A New Sacred*, later titled *Messiah*. Few people at this time appreciated the work, however, and in 1751 when Handel's sight began to fail, he wrote a beautiful oratorio with the words, "How dark, O Lord, are Thy decrees . . . all our joys to sorrow turning . . . as the night succeeds the day."

On April 14, 1759, a week before he died at age 74, Handel conducted the "Hallelujah Chorus" at a performance of *Messiah*. He was blind, but his face was aglow with joy as he directed the exuberant voices singing praises to the resurrected Lord. No longer in despair, Handel was filled with hope.

Like Handel, the twelve disciples went through a time of darkness and despair. During that last week with Jesus, their hopes were dashed as the One they wanted to crown King of Judea was tried, crucified, and buried. But their despair turned to rejoicing on that resurrection morning when Jesus Christ, King of kings, came forth from the grave victorious over death. He was indeed the final sacrifice, the Hope of all ages, the New Covenant, and the Life of the world.

I. THE PLAN REVEALED (MARK 14:1-26)

The air of Jerusalem was tense with excitement during Passover week. For months the Jewish religious leaders had plotted to kill Jesus, but they had decided He couldn't be arrested during Passover week. They feared the huge crowds. But man doesn't decide the timing for God's plans. God does. Three times Jesus had told the disciples that He would suffer, be rejected, die and rise. The time had come. Two events immediately foreshadowed the fulfillment of Jesus' words. First, Jesus was anointed at Bethany. And second, the Passover Feast became the Lord's Supper.

A. Jesus was anointed.

Jesus went to Bethany to eat a simple meal with friends. We know from John's Gospel that Mary, Martha, and their brother Lazarus, whom Jesus had raised from the dead, were there. Mary took a jar of very expensive perfume, broke the jar, and poured the perfume on Jesus' head. When someone protested, pointing out that the costly perfume could have been sold and the money given to the poor, Jesus said, *"You have the poor with you always . . . but Me you do not have always. She has done what she could. She has come beforehand to anoint My body for burial"* (Mark 14:7-8).

In contrast to Mary, Judas Iscariot, one of the 12 disciples, went to the chief priests and offered to betray Jesus for thirty pieces of silver.

B. The Passover Feast became the Lord's Supper.

On that Passover night when Jesus gathered His disciples around Him for the Passover Feast, He announced that one of them would betray Him. John's Gospel tells us that Judas Iscariot took the bread which Jesus gave him, a symbol of his betrayal, and departed to do his evil deed.

To those remaining, Jesus revealed the New Covenant. He identified His body and His blood as the body and blood of the final Passover lamb to be slain. The cup He offered them was a symbol of both suffering and joy—the two coming together for us today in the Lord's Supper.

After they sang a hymn, they went out to the Mount of Olives. Jesus yearned for His disciples to understand what was happening. But how could they understand that the Passover Feast observed for centuries foreshadowed God's great plan of redemption for mankind, the final Passover and sacrifice of this night?

When Mary poured expensive perfume on Jesus' head, He used the incident to teach His disciples. What did He teach them?

Explain in your own words how the Passover Feast revealed God's plan of salvation for men.

II. THE MESSIAH REJECTED (MARK 14:27-15:15)

A. Rejected by those close to Him

Perhaps the most painful rejection any of us ever face is rejection by those we love the most. Jesus surely felt the pain of being rejected by His disciples. Judas Iscariot and Peter were both close companions of Jesus, yet they were far apart in love for their Master. When Judas discovered that there was no financial gain in following Jesus, he turned traitor. He rejected Jesus and later betrayed him with a kiss—ironically a sign of love.

Peter's rejection was only temporary, but it was none the less painful for Jesus. Peter, along with the other disciples, was unable to stay awake while Jesus prayed in the Garden of Gethsemane. Three times Jesus awakened them, and three times they failed Him. Later after Jesus was arrested the disciples fled—all but Peter. He went as far as the courtyard, but there he denied his Master three times. Jesus had said that the cock would crow to remind Peter of his denial. When this happened, Peter broke down and wept.

B. Rejected by the Jewish religious leaders

The chief priests, elders and teachers of the law were the first group to question Jesus' authority. When Jesus arrived in Jerusalem for the Passover, they enlisted the Herodians and the Sadducees to help them trap the Rabbi who was usurping their authority.

The 72 men of the Sanhedrin before whom Jesus was tried, rejected Him and condemned Him because He answered the high priests truthfully. Caiaphas asked, *"Are You the Christ, the Son of the Blessed?"* And Jesus answered, *"I am. And you will see the Son of Man sitting at the right hand of the Power, and coming with the clouds of heaven"* (Mark 14:61-62). With boldness, Jesus was assuring the Sanhedrin that the day would come when He would judge them.

C. Rejected by the Roman governor, Pilate

The chief priests, elders, teachers of the law, and the whole Sanhedrin reached a decision: they took Jesus to Pilate and accused Him of treason against the Roman government. Pilate had his own inner struggle as he tried first to avoid an unpleasant issue, and second to escape responsibility. In the end, he chose not to stand up for Jesus—and thereby rejected Him.

D. Rejected by the crowd

Early in the morning, Pilate had a convicted murderer named Barabbas brought before the crowd. Roman custom decreed that the people could choose one prisoner to be released at Passover. The religious leaders had stirred up the crowd against Jesus, and the people shouted for Pilate to release Barabbas and crucify Jesus.

As we read the story of that dark night, we might well wonder why no one at all stood by Jesus. All who were close to Him were either asleep or in hiding. The rejection was complete. Jesus stood alone before His enemies.

EXPLORING

THE NEW TESTAMENT

_____
_____
_____
_____

_____
_____
_____
_____
_____
_____
_____
_____
_____
_____
_____
_____
_____
_____
_____
_____
_____
_____
_____
_____
_____
_____
_____

EXPLORING

What kept the religious leaders and Pilate from accepting Jesus as the Messiah?

_____
_____
_____
_____

Recall a time when, like Peter, you were weak and rejected Jesus. Briefly explain how you felt.

_____
_____
_____
_____

III. THE SACRIFICE MADE (MARK 15:16-47)

After beating and ridiculing Jesus, the Roman soldiers led Him out of the city to Golgotha and there they crucified Him. Jesus hung on the cross for three hours in the heat of the day suffering excruciating pain and agony. But the physical pain and the mental rejection which Jesus endured did not compare to His spiritual suffering. Jesus was the final sacrifice for man's sin, and the weight of that sin on One who had never known sin could only be borne by the Son of God. Hanging on the cross, mocked and insulted, Jesus suffered as no man can ever know when He cried out, *"Eloi, Eloi, lama sabachthani?"*—*"My God, My God, why have You forsaken Me?"* (Mark 15:34). Then death came to Jesus, and the curtain of the Temple was torn from top to bottom. No longer was man separated from God.

That evening before the Sabbath began, Joseph of Arimathea took the body of Jesus from the cross, wrapped it in fine linen, and placed it in a tomb cut out of rock. Then he rolled a stone across the entrance.

EXPLORING

Why did Jesus not answer the insults hurled at Him while He hung on the cross?

_____
_____
_____
_____

Explain the deepest suffering Jesus endured.

_____

_____

_____

_____

Why did the act of Joseph of Arimathea take great courage? Relate a time when you acted courageously for Jesus.

_____

_____

_____

_____

IV. THE HOPE SECURED (MARK 16)

Every year in Jerusalem thousands of grieving worshipers gather at the Church of the Holy Sepulcher on Easter morning. Then in the service, a hush falls over the crowd. The priest enters the rock-hewn tomb believed to be the place where Jesus' body was laid and comes out with a lighted candle, symbol of the resurrection. Joy breaks forth as the light is passed through the crowd and candles are lighted. Bells begin to peal and worshipers shout, "Christ is risen! Christ is risen!"

This was the message of the angel to Mary Magdalene and Mary the mother of James 2,000 years ago when they came to the garden to anoint the body of Jesus and found the tomb empty. God's plan of salvation was complete. The Lamb of God had been sacrificed for man's sin, and He had risen to conquer death. Later Jesus appeared to the disciples who had stubbornly refused to believe those who had seen Him earlier. He rebuked them and commanded them to _"Go into all the world and preach the gospel to every creature"_ (Mark 16:15). That is our task today. We are to go and tell the world the good news. Christ arose! Our hope for eternal life is secure!

What is the hope which Jesus secured for us by His victory over sin and death?

_____

_____

_____

_____

RESURRECTION APPEARANCES

Jesus appeared to:	Reference
1. Mary Magdalene	Mark 16:9-11; John 20:11-18
2. Several Women	Matthew 28:9-10
3. Two Disciples on the way to Emmaus	Mark 16:12-13; Luke 24:13-35
4. Peter	Luke 24:33-35; I Corinthians 15:5
5. Ten Disciples	Mark 16:14; Luke 24:36-43; John 20:19-25
6. Eleven Disciples	John 20:26-31; I Corinthians 15:5
7. Disciples by the Sea of Galilee	John 21:1-25
8. To Five Hundred People	I Corinthians 15:6
9. James, probably the Lord's brother	I Corinthians 15:7
10. Eleven Disciples	Matthew 28:16-20; Mark 16:14-18
11. Eleven Disciples at the Ascension	Mark 16:19-20; Luke 24:50-53; Acts 1:9-12
12. Apostle Paul on the road to Damascus	I Corinthians 15:8; Acts 9:3-5

SEARCH AND DECIDE

1. To add to your understanding of Mark 14:25, read Revelation 19:6-9. What did you learn?

_____

_____

_____

_____

_____

_____

_____

2. Read Mark 15:38 and Hebrews 10:11-23. When Jesus died on the cross the curtain in the Temple was torn from top to bottom. What difference does this make in your life today?

_____

_____

_____

_____

_____

_____

_____

_____

9

HEAR · ASK · OBEY

THE COMPASSIONATE, LOVING LORD

READING:
Luke

OBJECTIVES:
1. You will grasp an overview of the Gospel of Luke, its distinctive purpose, style, and content.
2. You will see Jesus Christ as the Savior who came to redeem us, and a compassionate, loving Lord.

THEME:
Jesus Christ, the compassionate, loving Lord

EXPLORING THE NEW TESTAMENT

Rosalind Rinker once wrote that God's love and voice came to her as she was reading the life story of J. Hudson Taylor, the founder of the China Inland Mission. "As I read some of his experiences with the Chinese," she wrote, "I was amazed that they were people like myself! My heart became involved, and I loved them."

God's love often touches us through the life stories of great men of faith. In God's Word we meet many Biblical characters who reveal God's love to us as we read of His faithfulness to them. This is true in the Gospel of Luke because it is a book of love. Luke is the most complete life story of Jesus that we have. His compassion and love permeate the numerous stories of people with whom He came into contact.

Matthew filled his Gospel with Old Testament references because he wanted the Jews to see Jesus as the long-expected Messiah. Mark stripped away everything that might take our attention off of Jesus so we could see Him as the Son of God, Savior of mankind, and follow Him. But Luke seldom quoted the Old Testament, and his Gospel was the longest and most complete of the four. Luke presented the compassionate, loving Lord who said to a poor widow, "Don't cry," and who said to the sinful woman as she anointed His feet with her tears, "Go in peace."

I. THE GOSPEL OF LUKE

A. Author (Luke 1:1-4)

Luke was a very active man who had a broad ministry. He was a doctor, teacher, missionary, pastor, historian and writer. He was well-educated and wrote fluent Greek. Not only was he acquainted with the disciples and leading Christians of his day, but he also knew important Roman officials. One of these was Theophilus to whom the Gospel of Luke and the Acts of the Apostles are both addressed.

B. Purpose

Luke's first book, the Gospel of Luke, focused on the life of Jesus Christ. His second book, Acts of the Apostles, focuses on the life of the early church. Luke wrote to instruct Theophilus in the

Christian faith, but he also wanted all men to know the love of Jesus whom he had come to know and serve. *"It seemed good to me also,"* Luke wrote, *"having had perfect understanding of all things from the very first, to write to you an orderly account"* (Luke 1:3)

C. Style

Luke's writing style was influenced by both his purpose and his personality. First, Luke was a historian. He knew he was reporting the most significant event in history and, more than the other Gospel writers, he dated important events. Second, Luke had a love and concern for people. At a time in history when women and children were given little attention, Luke chose to include many stories about them in his Gospel. He traced the genealogy of Jesus through Mary, included the infancy of Jesus and John, and recorded several miracles concerning children. Third, Luke didn't show partiality to any one group of people. He recognized that God had come to both Jew and Gentile, rich and poor, exalted and lowly. Fourth, Luke's vocabulary is rich and varied throughout. And he included four beautiful songs. But the beauty of his writing lies in the love and compassion of Jesus which shines through and touches the reader.

List three things you know about Luke, the man, which had an influence on his writing.

What was the original purpose of Luke's Gospel? What other purpose has it served?

II. THE LOVING LORD OF BOTH JEWS AND GENTILES (LUKE 1:5-24:44)

A. The coming and preparation of Jesus (Luke 1:5-4:13)

Only Luke recorded the story of the birth of John the Baptist, the forerunner of the Messiah. The angel Gabriel appeared to a faithful priest, Zechariah, and told him that his elderly wife, Elizabeth, would bear a son.

And Luke's story of the birth of Jesus has become familiar to all of us—the holy infant wrapped in cloths and placed in a manger; the angels singing "Glory to God in the highest"; the shepherds hurrying to Bethlehem to see the King of kings. We know nothing of Jesus' childhood except what Luke recorded.

At about age thirty, Jesus came to John to be baptized. Afterwards, *"filled with the Holy Spirit,"* Jesus was *"led by the Spirit into the wilderness,"* and tempted by the devil for forty days (Luke 4:1). Three times Jesus resisted the temptations by quoting Scripture—something we would do well to remember. Jesus' ministry had begun.

B. His ministry in and around Galilee (Luke 4:14-9:50)

Jesus began His ministry in Galilee. In Nazareth, His hometown, Jesus read from the scroll of Isaiah in the synagogue, but the people drove Him out of town. It's often difficult for us to explain to those closest to us what God has done in our lives.

Luke recorded more details about the calling of Jesus' disciples than did Matthew or Mark. He also placed the Sermon on the Mount immediately following the calling of the Twelve, and did not cover it in depth as Matthew did. But the Parable of the Sower is the same. Jesus continued to cast out demons, heal the sick, and preach the good news of the kingdom of God. He called on the Twelve to answer the question, "Who do you say that I am?" And He taught them that the Son of Man must suffer, be rejected, die and rise again.

C. His ministry in Judea and Perea (Luke 9:51-19:27)

Sixteen of the twenty-three parables found in Luke appear in this section. In addition, many of these parables are unique to this Gospel. Among these are the Parable of the Good Samaritan, The Rich Fool, The Lowest Seat at the Feast, The Lost Coin, The Prodigal Son, The Dishonest Manager, and the Persistent Widow.

Many people watched Jesus minister to blind beggars, lepers, and poor widows. They saw His gentleness with little children. And they saw the compassion and love of God in the Son of God who had come as their Messiah. But Jesus warned about the cost of being His disciple. The way into the kingdom of God is by a narrow door, He said, and not everyone will enter.

D. His final sacrifice and triumph in Jerusalem (Luke 19:28-24:44)

All four Gospel writers record the triumphal entry of Jesus into Jerusalem and His cleansing of the Temple. But only Luke shows us the love of Jesus for this holy city. Luke says Jesus wept over Jerusalem (Luke 19:41). In this City of David, Jesus shared the Passover Feast with His disciples. He explained the New Covenant which rested in Him alone. On that night Jesus gave to all believers symbols of His love and

EXPLORING

THE NEW TESTAMENT

57

_____

_____

_____

_____

_____

_____

_____

_____

_____

_____

_____

_____

_____

_____

_____

_____

_____

_____

_____

_____

_____

_____

_____

_____

_____

sacrifice: the cup, a symbol of His shed blood, and the bread, a symbol of His broken body.

Jesus was later arrested as He prayed on the Mount of Olives. After trials before Pilate and Herod, He was condemned to die. As Jesus was on the way to Golgotha, a large crowd followed Him, some of them women who were weeping. Jesus turned to them and said, *"Daughters of Jerusalem, do not weep for Me, but weep for yourselves and for your children"* (Luke 23:28).

Luke records three of the seven sayings of Jesus as He hung on the cross. Of the four Gospel writers, only Luke included Jesus' words to one of the two thieves who were crucified on either side of Him. As darkness came, about the sixth hour, Jesus committed His spirit to the Father.

Three days later, Jesus rose from the dead, and Luke wrote a joyful account of the women who found the empty tomb, and of Peter's quick dash there when he heard the news. Later, Jesus appeared to the disciples and others assembled with them. How eager Jesus was that they *know* Him and believe that He was alive.

Of the 23 parables in Luke, which one has the most meaning for you? Explain.

_____

_____

_____

_____

_____

SEVEN SAYINGS OF JESUS ON THE CROSS

1. *"Father, forgive them, for they do not know what they do."* Luke 23:34

2. *"Assuredly, I say to you, today you will be with me in Paradise."* Luke 23:43

3. *"Woman, behold your son! Behold your mother!"* John 19:26, 27

4. *"My God, My God, why have You forsaken Me?"* Matthew 27:46; Mark 15:34

5. *"I thirst."* John 19:28

6. *"It is finished!"* John 19:30

7. *"Father, into Your hands I commend My spirit."* Luke 23:46

List three characteristics of Jesus which you see clearly in Luke's Gospel. Give references for each.

_____

_____

_____

_____

_____

III. THE PROMISE AND THE BLESSING (LUKE 24:45-53)

Note the patience of Jesus as He *"opened their understanding, that they might comprehend the Scriptures"* (Luke 24:45). Everything that had happened had been part of God's plan, prophesied in the Scriptures. Then Jesus told them to *"tarry in the city of Jerusalem until you are endued with power from on high"* (Luke 24:49). The disciples could not do the task Jesus had for them alone.

Luke's description of Jesus' ascension into heaven is not one of sorrow or fear, but of peace and joy. Jesus blessed them, then *"they worshiped Him, and returned to Jerusalem with great joy"* (Luke 24:52). The Gospel of Luke began with joy and ended with joy. Within its pages we see Jesus, the Savior who came to redeem us, our compassionate, loving Lord.

What promise did Jesus make to His disciples in Luke 24:49? How does this promise affect us?

_____

_____

_____

_____

What evidence do you find that Luke's Gospel is one of joy?

_____

_____

_____

_____

_____

SEARCH AND DECIDE

1. Read Luke 1:1-4 and Acts 1:1-5. What did you learn?

_____

_____

_____

_____

_____

_____

_____

2. Paul mentions Luke in three of his letters: Colossians 4:14, Philemon 24, and II Timothy 4:11. What do you learn about Luke from these references?

_____

_____

_____

_____

_____

_____

_____

_____

10

HEAR · **ASK** · **OBEY**

JESUS: THE WORD OF LIFE

READING:
John 1-3

OBJECTIVES:
1. You will understand and appreciate John's purpose in writing his Gospel.
2. You will recognize the words and phrases John repeatedly uses and will grapple with their deeper meanings.
3. You will see Jesus, flesh and spirit, man and God, the Word of life.

THEMES:
Believe/Know	Light/Darkness
Signs/Works	Titles of Christ
Witness/Testimony	Numbers

As children, one of the first Bible verses many of us learned was *"Love one another,"* from the Gospel of John. Later we memorized John 3:16, one of the most quoted verses from the entire Bible: *"For God so loved the world. . . ."* And as adults, perhaps most of us have struggled with John 14:6, the words of Jesus declaring, *"No one comes to the Father except through me."*

The Gospel of John is written in simple language, so simple a child can read it. But the teaching is so rich that we can never plumb the depths of its meaning. This is true from the very first sentence. *"In the beginning was the Word, and the Word was with God, and the Word was God."* Only one word has more than one syllable, yet the meaning is awesome.

Traditionally, scholars have accepted John, the *"disciple whom Jesus loved,"* as the author of the Gospel of John, three letters—I, II, and III John—and The Revelation. It's possible that John and Jesus were cousins and knew each other during their growing-up years. Several verses in the Gospels lead us to believe that Mary the mother of Jesus, and Salome the mother of John were sisters. (See Matt. 27:56; Mark 15:40; and John 19:25.)

But when Jesus first called John to be His disciple, John was a boisterous, hot-tempered fisherman. He was attracted to Jesus, however, and slowly changed. On the cross, Jesus chose John to care for Mary, His mother.

Late in his life, while pastoring the church at Ephesus, John wrote his recollections of His beloved Lord. We believe his Gospel was written around A.D. 85-90, long after John's faith had been tried and tested.

His Gospel is different from the other three. Matthew's Gospel was written primarily for Jews, and is filled with Old Testament scriptures. John's Gospel was written for both Jew and Gentile, Christian and non-Christian. Luke was careful to date events, to give his story a historical foundation. John wasn't as interested in the sequence of events as he was in their significance. The Synoptic Gospels record much of the same material. John, on the other hand, didn't record the birth,

EXPLORING

THE NEW TESTAMENT

baptism, or temptations of Jesus, and he included no parables. Of the eight miracles which he did include, six are not found in the other Gospels.

More than the others, John's Gospel has the touch of an eyewitness. John remembered that the bread brought to Jesus to feed the 5,000 was *"five barley loaves"* (John 6:9). He remembered that Jesus *"spat on the ground,"* and *"made clay with the saliva,"* when healing a blind man (John 9:6). And he remembered that *"the house was filled with the fragrance of the oil"* when Mary anointed Jesus' feet at Bethany (John 12:3).

John stated the purpose of his writing clearly: *"But these are written that you may believe that Jesus is the Christ, the Son of God, and that believing you may have life in His name"* (John 20:31). John knew Jesus perhaps more intimately than anyone else. He wanted others to know Him as well.

I. THE WORD BECAME FLESH (JOHN 1:1-28)

John presented the Messiah to his readers as the eternal Word. The use of "Word" was not new to Biblical writings. John drew heavily on the Old Testament—God's Word active not only in creating but also in healing, in speaking to the prophets, bringing visions and judging. God is personified in His Word. His Word has power and authority.

But we get even more than personification when we read in John's Gospel, *"In the beginning was the Word, and the Word was with God, and the Word was God. He was in the beginning with God"* (John 1:1-2). We see a relationship—an intimate, personal relationship of the Word to God. The Word was not created; the Word was God. Then, *"The Word became flesh and dwelt among us"* (John 1:14). Now we get a sense of the intimate, personal relationship God desires to have with us. John wants us to believe this.

After this, the "Word" is not used in John's Gospel again in a personal sense. Instead, the Word appears as the very *Life* of mankind and as the *Light* which shines in the darkness of the world.

John also introduces the word "believe." The word is always a verb—an action word. We are to *"believe in his name."* John uses more than 30 different names (or titles) for the Messiah to teach us that Jesus Christ is the *"only begotten of the Father"* (John 1:14).

Don't confuse John the disciple and author with John the Baptist whose birth was announced by the angel Gabriel as the forerunner of the Messiah. John the Baptist announced the coming of Jesus, calling men to repent and be baptized. Because of his popularity, he could have become a false messiah—but he didn't. He knew his mission, and he never waivered from it. John the Baptist gave all power and authority and honor to Jesus. And so must we.

Make a list of facts given about the Word in verses 1-4.

_____

_____

_____

_____

What was the mission of John, the *"man who was sent from God"*?

_____

_____

_____

_____

II. AND MADE HIS DWELLING AMONG US. . . . (JOHN 1:29-2:25)

A. Jesus came to John the Baptist.

When John the Baptist saw Jesus approaching, he said, *"Behold! The Lamb of God who takes away the sin of the world!"* (John 1:29). Jesus was to be the Passover lamb, the final sacrifice. He would pay the price for man's sin.

God gave John the Baptist a special sign so that he would recognize the Christ. The Spirit came down from heaven and remained on Jesus. The dove was a symbol of new life, and Mosaic law also accepted it as suitable for sacrifice. Both these meanings pointed to the work of Jesus. In addition, Jesus was to baptize with the Holy Spirit. John testified that Jesus was the Son of God.

B. Jesus gathered His first disciples.

Two of John the Baptist's disciples followed Jesus. We believe one of them was John, the author of the Gospel; the other was Andrew. Andrew went in search of his brother, Simon, and brought him to Jesus. Jesus changed Simon's name to Peter, a name which means "rock." The following day Jesus called Philip, and Philip brought Nathanael. Jesus was gathering His disciples.

C. Jesus performed the first miraculous sign.

There are no parables in the Gospel of John, but the eight miracles included are meant to teach just as parables teach. John saw the miracles as signs which confirmed the truth that Jesus was the Son of God.

The first of these signs took place at a wedding in Cana which Jesus attended. When all the wine was gone, Jesus had

the servants fill six stone jars with water, and He changed the water into wine. As a miracle, the sign revealed the glory of the Son of God, and *"His disciples believed in Him"* (John 2:11).

MIRACLES, OR MIRACULOUS SIGNS, IN JOHN'S GOSPEL

Sign	Reference
1. Changing water into wine at a wedding in Cana.	John 2:1-11
2. Healing the son of a Roman official.	John 4:46-54
3. Healing the invalid by the pool of Bethesda.	John 5:1-14
4. Feeding the 5,000 (Appears in all four Gospels.)	John 6:1-15
5. Walking on the water. (Appears in Matt., Mark, John)	John 6:16-24
6. Giving sight to a man born blind.	John 9:1-41
7. Raising Lazarus from the dead.	John 11:1-46
8. Catching fish in the Sea of Tiberias.	John 21:1-8

D. Jesus cleansed the Temple.

God has always intended that His house would be *"a house of prayer for all nations"* (Isaiah 56:7). But the Temple was in great need of cleansing. When Jesus saw that it had been turned into a market, He took a whip and drove out the moneychangers and merchants selling animals for sacrifice.

The Jews demanded, *"What sign do You show to us, since You do these things?"* (John 2:18). Jesus' thoughts had turned to a spiritual temple—His body. If destroyed, Jesus said, He would raise it again in three days. The Jews didn't understand. Neither did the disciples—until after He was raised from the dead.

What evidence do you see in John 1:29-34 that Jesus is the expected Messiah?

From your observation of Jesus in John 1:35-51 what three words would you use to describe Him as He relates to people?

_____

_____

_____

_____

Compare the response of the servants in John 2:7-8 with the response of the Jews to Jesus in John 2:15-20. With which group do you identify?

_____

_____

_____

_____

III. FULL OF GRACE AND TRUTH (JOHN 3)

Nicodemus was a member of the Sanhedrin. He saw some of the miraculous signs Jesus was doing among the people of Jerusalem during Passover week. He was interested and wanted to know more about Jesus.

When we see the miraculous works of God today, we are always faced with a decision: Will we believe that the miracle was the work of God—or not? When Nicodemus saw the signs, his heart was open. For him, the signs pointed to God. Seeing the sincerity of Nicodemus, Jesus explained to Him that *"unless one is born again, he cannot see the kingdom of God"* (John 3:3). Like many of us, Nicodemus thought of physical things while Jesus spoke of spiritual things. Nicodemus was a religious leader, yet he had missed the way and his heart was empty. Jesus saw that Nicodemus, like so many *"lost sheep of Israel,"* was walking in darkness. And Jesus was the *Light*. Jesus' words were full of love and compassion: *"For God so loved the world that He gave His only begotten Son, that whoever believes in Him should not perish but have everlasting life"* (John 3:16).

William How, a nineteenth century hymn writer, joined with John the Apostle in praise to Jesus, the Word of Life:

> O Word of God Incarnate
> O Wisdom from on high,
> O Truth unchanged, unchanging,
> O Light of our dark sky:
> We praise Thee for the radiance
> That from the hallowed page,
> A lantern to our footsteps,
> Shines on from age to age.

EXPLORING

THE NEW TESTAMENT

65

Read John 3:16-17 as a personal message, substituting "me" for "world." Begin: "For God so loved me . . ." How do you respond?

What is the relationship of "believe" to the symbols of light/darkness in John's Gospel?

TITLES OF JESUS USED IN THE GOSPEL OF JOHN

References are to first time use only. John must have used these many titles to help his reader see the deity of Jesus Christ.

1. Word 1:1
2. Light 1:7
3. Jesus Christ 1:17
4. Son 1:18
5. Lord 1:23
6. One 1:26
7. Lamb of God 1:29
8. Man 1:30
9. Son of God 1:34
10. Jesus 1:37
11. Rabbi 1:38
12. Messiah 1:41
13. Jesus of Nazareth 1:45
14. King of Israel 1:49
15. Son of Man 3:13
16. Bridegroom 3:29
17. Prophet 4:19
18. Savior 4:42
19. Bread of life 6:35
20. Living bread 6:51
21. Christ 6:9
22. Teacher 8:4
23. Light 8:12
24. I AM 8:58
25. Door of the sheep ... 10:7
26. Good shepherd 10:11
27. God 10:30, 33
28. Resurrection .... 11:25 and the life
29. The way, the .... 14:6 truth, and the life
30. True vine 15:1
31. Vine 15:5
32. Your Son 17:1
33. King of the Jews 18:33
34. King 18:37
35. Rabboni 20:16

SEARCH AND DECIDE

1. Read Genesis 1:1-2 and John 1:1-2. What truths about God do you find from a comparison of these verses?

_____

_____

_____

_____

_____

_____

_____

_____

2. Many incidents in the Bible are a foreshadowing of things to come and often have deeper meaning than the incident itself. Compare John 3:14-15 with Numbers 21:4-9. What did you learn?

_____

_____

_____

_____

_____

_____

_____

_____

HEAR / ASK

11

OBEY

JESUS: GIVER AND SUSTAINER OF LIFE

READING:
John 4-7

OBJECTIVES:
1. You will see Jesus as the One who can fulfill all our expectations.
2. You will see Jesus as the giver and sustainer of life.

THEMES:

Believe/Know	Light/Darkness
Signs/Works	Titles of Christ
Witness/Testimony	Life/Death

John Updike wrote a short story about a young boy named Ben who excitedly waited all day for the carnival to open. That night, clutching a 50-cent piece in his hand, Ben hurried toward the bright lights and carnival music. He worked his way through the crowd of people and stopped to watch a thickset man with rolled-up shirt sleeves twirl a tinselled wheel. But no one playing the game won. When Ben lost his nickels one by one, a man with a blue fish, an anchor, and the word "peace" tattooed on his arm, gave him back two coins. Ben took the coins and, feeling empty and cheated, left the carnival with a cone of cotton candy. It was sweet in his mouth but was gone before he reached home. And tomorrow the carnival would move on.[1]

Many people are like Ben. They go through life building up expectations of what the carnivals of the world have to offer, only to have their hopes of finding the "real thing" dashed again and again.

Jesus came to point us to God who alone can fulfill all our expectations and give us lasting peace and rest. He came as a bright light into our world of darkness to bring us *life*.

Many people in John's day watched in amazement as Jesus performed miracles, but they went away unchanged. John won't allow us to do that. He saw the miraculous signs of Jesus as symbols pointing to spiritual truths. So must we. To keep us focused on what Jesus was teaching, this lesson will draw your attention to seven things Jesus said. Each one evolved from a literal situation, but Jesus spoke on a spiritual level.

John's Gospel must be thoughtfully read on two levels—the literal and the symbolic. As you read, watch for the six key themes in this lesson and carefully consider the deeper meaning of each.

I. "NEVER THIRST AGAIN" (JOHN 4:1-42)

In the first century, Jews seldom passed through Samaria to go to Galilee. Hatred between Samaritans and Jews took root about 722 B.C. when Assyria swept into Israel and took

EXPLORING

THE NEW TESTAMENT

thousands captive. The Assyrians moved many captives from other conquered nations into Israel and renamed the land Samaria. The Samaritans accepted only the Pentateuch, but awaited the coming of a Messiah.

Jesus was tired, hungry, and thirsty when he arrived at Jacob's well in Sychar. He sent the disciples into the town to buy food, and then sat down to rest. But a Samaritan woman came to the well, and Jesus began to minister to her. What can we learn from Jesus' ministry to this Samaritan woman?

First, the story is a model for us to follow in presenting the Gospel. Jesus accepted the woman just as she was and met her on her own ground. Second, He made it clear that the living water He offered was for people of all nations and races. Third, Jesus was speaking of the promised Holy Spirit when He said, *"Whoever drinks of the water that I shall give him will never thirst"* (John 4:14).

What can you learn from the story of the Samaritan woman that will help you lead others to Christ?

Recall the questions you had when you first began to realize who Jesus was. Write them down. Do you think you felt anything like the Samaritan woman?

II. "YOUR SON LIVES" (JOHN 4:43-54)

Jesus had performed the first of the seven miraculous signs which John recorded when He had changed water into wine at a wedding feast in Cana. Now in Cana again, Jesus performed the second miraculous sign by giving life to the son of a Roman official.

When the official came to Jesus, he wasn't thinking of signs. He came begging Jesus to heal his son. *"Sir,"* he said, *"come down before my child dies!"* And Jesus replied, *"Go your way; your son lives"* (John 4:49-50).

The man's servant met him on the road and told him the boy was well. And this miraculous sign pointed the man and all his household to God. They believed. Remember: the word "believe" is always an action word in John's Gospel.

What brought the Roman official to faith in Jesus? What did you see in Jesus which caused you to believe in Him?

_____

_____

_____

_____

III. "YOU HAVE BEEN MADE WELL. SIN NO MORE" (JOHN 5:1-14)

The third miraculous sign occurred later when Jesus returned to Jerusalem for a Jewish feast. A multitude of invalids were lying around the pool of Bethesda. We don't know why Jesus chose to heal the one man who had been an invalid for 38 years. Whatever the reason, Jesus asked him, _"Do you want to be made well?"_ This was a good question. When we are content to stay as we are, Jesus can't change us. The man was willing. He wanted to be healed. When Jesus said, _"Rise, take up your bed and walk,"_ the man obeyed at once (John 5:6, 8). Notice that it was the Sabbath and the man went to the Temple. When Jesus found him there later, He said to him, _"See, you have been made well. Sin no more, lest a worse thing come upon you"_ (John 5:14)

Then the man knew it was Jesus who had healed him, and he shared the news with the Jews. But the Jews reminded him that he was breaking the law by carrying his bed on the Sabbath. Unlike the legalistic Jews, Jesus was concerned about the deep spiritual condition of the man, and this brought a confrontation.

Explain what you think Jesus meant when He said to the man He healed, "See you have been made well. Sin no more."

_____

_____

_____

_____

IV. "THOSE WHO HEAR WILL LIVE" (JOHN 5:15-47)

All the themes of John come together in this powerful answer which Jesus gave to the Jews when they questioned His use of the Sabbath. First, He called God *"Father."* To the Jews this was *"making Himself equal with Go."* (John 5:18). Second, Jesus claimed that the Father had given Him the authority to give *life* and to judge. Every Jew knew that only God could raise men from the dead and give life, and they acknowledged no judge but God. Jesus was speaking to those living in darkness, spiritually dead.

Those who heard Jesus make these claims were confronted with two alternatives: accept Jesus as the Messiah, the Son of God or reject Him as a blasphemer. People today face the same two alternatives. When we *hear* and *believe* Jesus, we cross over into His kingdom. In that moment, we move from spiritual death into *life* eternal.

EXPLORING

What are some of the things which kept many of the Jews from coming to Jesus that He might give them *life*? Put a check by those things on your list which can keep people from Jesus today.

V. "I AM THE BREAD OF LIFE" (JOHN 6:1-15, 25-71)

Jesus and His disciples were at Bethesda. The Passover Feast was near and many of those gathered around Jesus were on their way to Jerusalem. Jesus asked Philip, *"Where shall we buy bread, that these may eat?"* (John 6:5). Andrew knew a boy in the crowd who had five barley loaves and two small fish. Jesus took these and fed 5,000 people—the fourth miraculous sign. Everyone was satisfied, and twelve baskets of food were gathered up after the meal.

Many decided that Jesus was a prophet who had come to free them from Roman rule. And with Jesus' power to feed them, they would never again go hungry! But Jesus yearned to move their thinking from the physical to the spiritual. *"Do not labor for the food which perishes,"* He said, *"but for the food which endures to everlasting life, which the Son of Man will give you"* (John 6:27). Jesus was no doubt thinking of Himself as the Passover lamb when He said, *"The bread that I shall give is My flesh. . . . Unless you eat the flesh of the Son of Man and drink His blood, you have no life in you"* (John 6:51, 53). Some said His teaching was hard, but Jesus said the words were *"spirit"* and *"life."* Once more the choice was laid before those who heard Jesus.

What did Jesus want the disciples to learn when He fed the 5,000? What does He want you to learn?

_____

_____

_____

_____

VI. "IT IS I; DO NOT BE AFRAID"
(JOHN 6:16-24)

The fifth miraculous sign recorded by John pointed the disciples to the One who could relieve all their fears and whose presence today gives us peace.

The disciples learned this truth when they were crossing the Sea of Galilee and a storm came up. The waters were rough, and they were having a hard time rowing. We can't be sure whether they were more terrified of the storm or of what they thought was a ghost approaching them, walking on the water. But Jesus called out to them, *"It is I; do not be afraid"* (John 6:20). These were comforting words.

Those of us who have been involved in fearful situations, know what it is to be afraid. But in those times many have known the presence of Jesus and heard His words, *"Do not be afraid."* The opposite of fear is faith.

List three things you fear. We know our Lord does not want us to fear. Bow your head and ask Jesus to take away your fear.

_____

_____

_____

_____

_____

VII. "COME TO ME AND DRINK" (JOHN 7)

Jesus went alone and in secret to Jerusalem for the Jewish Feast of Tabernacles. But He went into the Temple court and began to teach, calling those who heard His words to either accept Him as the One who had come from God or reject

73

_____
_____
_____
_____
_____

_____
_____
_____
_____
_____
_____
_____
_____
_____
_____
_____
_____
_____
_____
_____
_____
_____
_____
_____
_____
_____
_____
_____
_____
_____
_____
_____
_____
_____
_____

Him. *"If anyone thirsts,"* Jesus said, *"let him come to Me and drink"* (John 7:37).

Today, the light of Jesus still shines in our dark world, a world which offers only "carnivals." And our Lord is still calling all who will *hear* to come and drink of the Living Water that they may never thirst, and eat of the Bread of Life that they may never again be hungry.

What do you see in Jesus' character that keeps Him moving toward His goal of changing man's sentence of death to eternal life?

_____
_____
_____
_____
_____

[1] "You'll Never Know, Dear, How Much I Love You," in *Pigeon Feathers and Other Stories* (Greenwich, Conn: Fawcett, 1959), pp. 120–124.

SEARCH AND DECIDE

1. Can people study the Bible and know what it teaches without finding *life* in Christ Jesus? Read the following to help you decide: John 5:24-47; 6:45-71 and II Corinthians 3:14-16.

_____

_____

_____

_____

_____

_____

_____

_____

2. Read Isaiah 55:1-3. In what way do these verses relate to John 4-7? Why do you think the bread and water symbols are found in both Isaiah and in John?

_____

_____

_____

_____

_____

_____

_____

_____

12

HEAR · ASK · OBEY

JESUS: LIGHT OF THE WORLD

READING:
John 8:1-11:54

OBJECTIVES:
1. You will understand the symbolism of light and darkness.
2. You will see the clear division between God's kingdom and Satan's kingdom.
3. You will confirm the words of Jesus as truth which can lead us from darkness into the light of His fellowship.

THEMES:
Believe/Know	Light/Darkness
Signs/Works	Titles of Christ
Witness/Testimony	Life/Death

EXPLORING THE NEW TESTAMENT

The Feast of Tabernacles and the Feast of Dedication are the background for Jesus' declaration, *"I am the light of the world"* and His teaching which followed. (John 8:12). During the Feast of Tabernacles, which took place at the end of the harvest in the fall, the large golden lampstands were lighted and flooded the Temple courtyard with light. The Feast of Dedication, which took place several weeks later, was often called the Festival of Lights. Today it's known as Hanukkah. This celebration commemorated the rededication of the Temple by Judas Maccabaeus in 165 B.C. At that time the beautiful Menorah, the pure gold lampstand with seven lamps molded together, was lighted—with only enough oil to burn one night. However, legend said that God miraculously caused the lamp to give light for eight days and nights.

Light and darkness are frequently used symbols in Scripture. If we are to understand John's Gospel, we must give attention not only to the literal events He records, but also to their deeper, symbolic meaning. In the beginning God separated the light from the darkness. From that point in Scripture light relates to good, darkness to evil. The kingdom of God is the kingdom of light; the kingdom of Satan is the kingdom of darkness. To believe the words of Jesus is to come to the Light. To disbelieve is to remain in darkness. John said the *"true Light which gives light to every man"* had come into the world and was shining *"in the darkness"* (John 1:9, 5).

Now in His last year of ministry, Jesus used light not only as a symbol for Himself when He said, *"I am the light of the world,"* but also as a sign of the works of God. John, too, saw each of the seven miracles he recorded as signs pointing to God in Christ Jesus. Each miracle showed the way out of darkness into light. The last two signs are in this lesson— the healing of the blind man and the raising of Lazarus.

Of the seven great "I Am" statements of Jesus, four are in this lesson: *"I am the light of the world," "I am the door," "I am the good shepherd,"* and *"I am the resurrection and the life"* (John 8:12; 10:9, 11; 11:25).

I. LIGHT IS THE OPPOSITE OF DARKNESS (JOHN 8)

Jesus came to the Temple courts at dawn, perhaps while the lamps in the courtyard were still burning for the Feast of Tabernacles. The Pharisees were also up early and managed to catch a woman in adultery. Moses' Law said she should be stoned, but Roman law didn't allow Jews to pronounce the death penalty. The Pharisees were trying to trap Jesus. However, He didn't condemn the woman. Rather, He stooped and wrote something on the ground, then stood and turned to the Pharisees. *"He who is without sin among you,"* He said, *"let him throw a stone at her first"* (John 8:7). One by one the Pharisees walked away—preferring to remain in their darkness.

What about the woman? Jesus was compassionate and refused to condemn her. He said to her, *"Go and sin no more"* (John 8:11). Although we do not hear anything more of her, we suspect that she obeyed Jesus. Surely the light of Jesus' face was more attractive to her than the darkness of her world of sin.

But we do hear more about the Pharisees. When Jesus said, *"I am the light of the world,"* they challenged His claim, and He gave them a lesson in relationships. *"You know neither Me nor My Father,"* Jesus said (John 8:19). The Pharisees were furious because they were descendants of Abraham. But Jesus reminded them that they were not doing the things Abraham did; they did not believe the truth. *"You are of your father the devil,"* Jesus said (John 8:44). The Light was shining in their midst, but they chose to remain in darkness.

Try to put yourself in the place of the woman caught in adultery. Which would be more likely to turn you from sin: the attitude of Jesus toward you or the attitude of the Pharisees? What can you learn from this?

Why did Jesus say being a descendant of Abraham didn't make the Pharisees God's children? What did Jesus say was the mark of one who belongs to God?

II. LIGHT IS SEEING AND BELIEVING (JOHN 9)

Some time between the Feast of Tabernacles and the Feast of Dedication (or Festival of Lights), Jesus and His disciples were walking down a street in Jerusalem when they saw a blind man. Jesus must have healed many blind people, but John chose to record the story of this one as the sixth "sign" that Jesus was the Messiah, the Son of God. Only a short time before Jesus had declared Himself to be the Light of the world. Now Jesus turned to the work before Him—to bring light out of this blind man's darkness.

The disciples watched as Jesus spat on the ground, made some mud with the saliva, and put it on the man's eyes. Then Jesus told him to go wash in the Pool of Siloam. The man obeyed and received his sight.

Note the different responses of the Pharisees, the parents of the blind man, and the blind man himself to this miracle. The Pharisees denounced Jesus because He healed a man on the Sabbath. The parents feared the Pharisees and shifted responsibility to their son. But the man Jesus healed grew stronger and came closer to Jesus with each question he answered.

In what ways does the opening of the blind man's eyes parallel your own experience in coming to know Jesus?

III. LIGHT IS LISTENING AND FOLLOWING THE GOOD SHEPHERD (JOHN 10)

When Jesus came, He said, *"I am the good shepherd"* and *"I am the door of the sheep"* (John 10:14, 7). Let's ask two questions to help us understand what Jesus is teaching.

First, are all shepherds good? No. Jesus called bad shepherds who came before Him *"thieves and robbers"* (John 10:8). One way of recognizing a good shepherd, Jesus said, is to *listen* to his voice. He calls his sheep by name, and they *follow* him. Our good Shepherd loved His sheep so much that He gave His life for His sheep.

Second, is there more than one door into the safety of the sheepfold? Jesus said no, and declared, *"I am the door of the shee."* (John 10:7). This must have angered the Jews just as it angers many people today who do not see Jesus as the only door into His kingdom.

THE NEW TESTAMENT

Today, "thieves and robbers" are still leading many people away from the good Shepherd. But those who *listen* to His words and *follow* Him will not be led astray.

In what way can the Pharisees be compared to the "thieves and robbers" Jesus talked about?

Could someone identify you as one who belongs to the good Shepherd? Why or why not?

IV. LIGHT IS COMING OUT OF DARKNESS. (JOHN 11:1-54)

The seventh miraculous sign, found only in the Gospel of John, is the raising of Lazarus from the dead. Jesus left Jerusalem after the Feast of Dedication, and went up to Perea because the Jews were trying to kill Him. For this reason, the urgency of His mission to bring light to men who lived in darkness was still weighing heavily on His mind when He received the news that his friend Lazarus was sick.

Lazarus, Mary and Martha lived in Bethany about two miles from Jerusalem and Jesus often visited their home. He loved them. But He waited two days after receiving the news of Lazarus' illness before beginning His journey to Bethany, and by that time, Lazarus had died. Why did He wait?

Jesus knew His friend would die. But He also knew He would bring him back to life as a sign of the power of God over death. When Jesus and His disciples arrived in Bethany, Martha came out to meet Jesus on the road. Note her trust and faith in Jesus, and her belief in the resurrection. Jesus said to her:

"I am the resurrection and the life. He who believes in Me, though he may die, he shall live. Do you believe this?"

John 11:25-26

Martha replied that she did indeed believe that He was the Christ, the Son of God, but it is doubtful that she understood that Jesus would raise Lazarus.

Jesus knew the condition of mankind, the darkness which sin had brought into the world. But could He make man understand that He was the Light which could dispel their darkness? Death was His enemy—a part of the "darkness" and the "night." And Jesus came to bring life and light to man.

Standing before the dark tomb of Lazarus, Jesus prayed to the Father. Then He called, "Lazarus, come forth!" The dead man, bound with strips of linen, came out of the darkness of the tomb into the light. Jesus, the Light of the world, had given him life.

Note how those who witnessed this miracle responded to Jesus. Many believed in Him, but others plotted to take His life.

What evidence can you find that Martha had great faith in Jesus even before He raised Lazarus from the dead?

_____

_____

_____

_____

Why do you think Jesus wept? What might cause Jesus to weep today?

_____

_____

_____

_____

Jesus is still the *light* of our dark world. His light shines through the lives of believers who *hear* the voice of the good Shepherd and follow Him.

As His light shines through us, the world will come to know that the darkness is passing away because His light is shining.

SEARCH AND DECIDE

1. Read the words of David from the following Psalms. David felt the light of God personally. Write out the verses which are personal to you. Psalm 27:1; 36:9; 56:13; 89:15.

_____

_____

_____

_____

_____

_____

_____

_____

2. Read the following and jot down the additional things you learn about light as the symbol relates to Jesus' words, "*I am the light. . . .*" Isaiah 9:2; 60:19; Micah 7:8–9; I Peter 2:9

_____

_____

_____

_____

_____

_____

_____

_____

JESUS: THE WAY, THE TRUTH, AND THE LIFE

John 11:55-16:33

OBJECTIVES:
1. You will see Jesus setting the example which those who serve Him must follow.
2. You will learn with the disciples as Jesus teaches that He is the Way, the Truth, and the Life.
3. You will be encouraged in your own ministry.

THEMES:
Believe/Know	Light/Darkness
Truth/Life	Love/Hate

In his story, "The Making of a Minister," Walter Wangerin, Jr. describes a man named Arthur who "had a walk and a manner like a toad, a high-backed slouch, and a burping contempt for his fellow parishioners." Arthur lived in a damp, filthy room crawling with roaches and pungent with the odor of cigarettes and mold.

It became the unpleasant duty of the minister, to visit Arthur, to listen to him dispute the young clergyman's faith, and in the later stages of Arthur's illness, to dress and care for him. In those difficult months before his death, Arthur demanded more and more time and service—with no promise of reward. But he taught the young minister, who came to love him, the meaning of sacrificial love, a Christ-like love, and prepared him for his ministry.

Jesus demonstrated in unexpected ways the kind of sacrificial love He wanted His disciples to have. He knew He faced death when He went to Jerusalem for the Passover Feast and presented Himself once again to the people as their Messiah. Afterwards, He drew His disciples away that He might spend His last few hours on earth teaching them the cost of following Him in His mission. He wanted them to know that He was indeed *"the way and the truth and the life"* (John 14:6) And He wanted them to know how much He loved them, and how much they must love each other. Their comfort and encouragement in the days ahead would come from the Holy Spirit whom Jesus promised to send.

I. KNOW THE COST (JOHN 11:55-12:50)

It was six days before the Passover, and Jesus knew that the hour of His death was approaching. He was in Bethany with His disciples, and Mary and Martha were giving a dinner in His honor. To express her love for Jesus, Mary took some very costly oil and poured it on Jesus feet, wiping His feet with her hair. Judas Iscariot was angry and asked why the oil was not sold and the money given to the poor. Satan was already working in his heart. But Jesus said Mary had anointed Him for His burial. *"The poor you have*

EXPLORING THE NEW TESTAMENT

with you always," Jesus said, "but Me you do not have always" (John 12:8).

The next day Jesus rode into Jerusalem, seated on a donkey, and heard the crowds shout, "Hosanna!" Joy was all around Him, but Jesus was sorrowful because He knew that few understood the terrible cost of their sin. They didn't understand His mission. The crowd wanted a king who could multiply bread and feed them. The Pharisees rejected Him as their Messiah because they didn't want to give up their power. The disciples were puzzled. And the Greeks came to see Him because they were curious. Did anyone understand?

Jesus began to teach the disciples that He must die, and that the cost of following Him was the same. He explained that unless a grain of wheat falls into the ground and dies, it will not produce more grain. "If anyone serves Me, let him follow Me," Jesus said, "where I am, there My servant will be also" (John 12:26). That is the cost of following Jesus. But by giving up our lives, Jesus said, we save them for eternal life.

Mary expressed her love for Jesus by pouring perfume on His feet. What are some ways we can express our love for Jesus?

_____

_____

_____

_____

_____

Read John 12:23-26. What relationship does the kernel of wheat have to Jesus and His ministry? What does it have to do with you?

_____

_____

_____

_____

II. ACCEPT THE MISSION (JOHN 13)

Following the Passover meal, and just prior to His arrest in Jerusalem, Jesus called His disciples to accept the mission of servanthood. He taught them what being a part of His ministry was all about by becoming a servant Himself. The disciples watched as Jesus rose from the table, removed his colorful robe, and wrapped a towel around His waist. Assuming the role of a lowly servant, Jesus began to wash the disciples' feet.

If someone you love and admire has ever knelt before you and washed your feet, you may be able to understand in a small way how Peter felt when Jesus knelt to wash his feet. Peter protested because he felt that a famous rabbi and teacher should not be doing such things. But Jesus wanted His disciples to learn that *"a servant is not greater than his master"* (John 13:16). Those who serve Jesus are called to be servants.

Judas didn't accept the mission of servanthood, and left to perform his treachery. But Jesus continued to teach those who remained. He commanded them to love one another just as He had loved them. This love was to be the mark of belonging to Jesus—the mark of His followers down through the ages.

Jesus had told the disciples that He was leaving them, that He must die. But Peter did not understand. Peter must have felt his love for Jesus well up inside of him as he asked, *"Lord, why can I not follow you now? I will lay down my life for your sake"* (John 13:37). But Jesus knew Peter's heart just as He knows ours when we sometimes make foolish statements. Peter was silent when Jesus told him that before the rooster crowed he would deny Him three times.

What was Jesus teaching the disciples when He washed their feet?

_____

_____

_____

_____

_____

In what ways do we *"wash one another's feet?"*

_____

_____

_____

_____

III. BELIEVE THE WORD (JOHN 14)

Jesus sensed that the disciples' hearts were troubled, and He offered words of comfort. Today, these words from John 14 still comfort believers in times of grief. Jesus explained that He was going to His Father's house to prepare a place for those who chose to follow Him. Someday, He said, He would return and take them to live with Him forever.

Jesus was speaking on a spiritual level when He said, *"I am the way, the truth, and the life. No one comes to the Father except through me"* (John 14:6). Jesus made it clear that He was the only way, the only bridge by which man might cross from eternal death to eternal life.

Jesus wanted the disciples to understand not only the unity of the Father, the Son, and the Holy Spirit, but also the unity believers were to have with God. Today, as believers, we can perhaps understand these truths even better than the disciples could at that moment. But after Pentecost the disciples would believe the words of Jesus as they experienced the love of God manifested through the Holy Spirit within them. The Holy Spirit within believers today is evidence that we have received *Life* and are *"in Christ Jesus."* God's Spirit opens our minds and hearts to understand the teachings of Jesus that we may obey them.

 In your own words, briefly explain what Jesus meant when He said, *"I am the way, the truth, and the life."*

IV. RELY ON THE HOLY SPIRIT (JOHN 15-16)

A pastor in central California kept his staff in a study of John 15 for almost a year. Indeed, the truth of these words of Jesus is so profound and so powerful that we will never be the same—if we hear. Jesus said:

"I am the vine, you are the branches. He who abides in Me, and I in him, bears much fruit; for without Me you can do nothing."

John 15:5

Fruit is the mark of a Christian. Jesus said one who belongs to Him WILL bear fruit. It isn't an alternative. Fruit for the Christian means two things. First, it's personal growth. We become more loving, joyful, peaceful, long suffering, kind, good, faithful, gentle, and self-controlled. (See Galatians 5:22-23.) Second, it's new believers. We bring others to Christ.

But these marks don't become ours through our own efforts. We must remain close to Christ. The life of the branches is in the vine. The life of believers is in Christ.

Jesus warned the disciples that such a life wouldn't be easy. They could expect persecution—even death. But He promised to send the Holy Spirit to be the constant companion of believers. As believers today, we have the Spirit to guide us, teach us, and comfort us as we live out our lives in a hostile world.

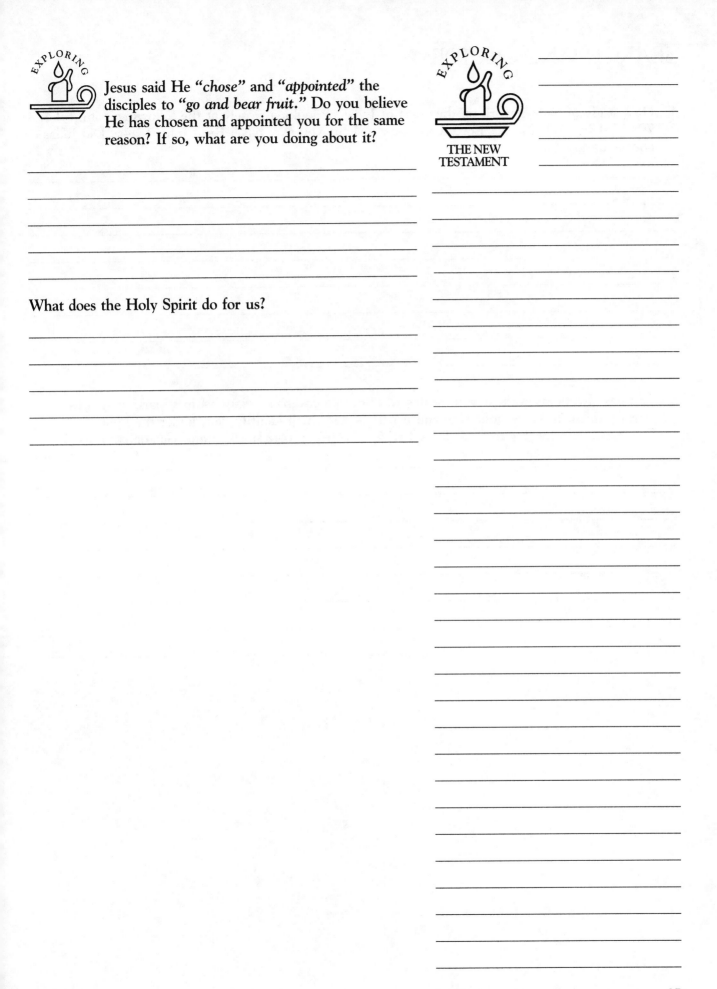

EXPLORING

Jesus said He *"chose"* and *"appointed"* the disciples to *"go and bear fruit."* Do you believe He has chosen and appointed you for the same reason? If so, what are you doing about it?

_____

_____

_____

_____

_____

What does the Holy Spirit do for us?

_____

_____

_____

_____

_____

EXPLORING

THE NEW
TESTAMENT

SEARCH AND DECIDE

1. Do a study of Satan's work on the heart of Judas by looking closely at the following: John 6:64, 70; 12:4-6; 13:2, 27, 30. Record any new insights you may have. Read John 12:46. Did Judas choose darkness?

_____

_____

_____

_____

_____

_____

_____

_____

2. God has always given those who belong to Him in a covenant relationship a mark or sign to identify them. Read the following and list the signs which identify you, under the New Covenant, as belonging to God: John 13:35; 14:16-17; 14:23; 15:5; and Galatians 5:22-25.

_____

_____

_____

_____

_____

_____

_____

_____

14

HEAR · ASK · OBEY

JESUS: THE LAMB OF GOD

READING:
John 17-19

OBJECTIVES:
1. You will see Jesus, full of love and compassion for man, in complete submission to the Father's plan.
2. You will see Jesus rejected by those He came to serve.
3. You will see Jesus as the Lamb of God.

THEMES:
Glory   Truth/Life
Believe/Know   Sacrifice
Light/Darkness

Ignatius, who served as bishop of the church at Antioch during the latter part of the first century, was martyred in Rome. On his way there, he was chained to a detachment of soldiers whom he described as a pack of leopards. Ignatius wrote that they enjoyed their "role as hunters, with me as their prey." But this suffering, Ignatius felt, would prepare him spiritually and mentally to face the lions in Rome. His devotion to Jesus Christ and his courage in facing death are evident in the seven letters which he wrote to churches on his way to Rome.

Almost a century later, Polycarp, bishop of Smyrna, was called before the governor who pleaded with him to "swear by the luck of Caesar" and denounce Jesus Christ. But Polycarp refused. "Eighty and six years have I served him," he said, "and he has done me no wrong. How then can I blaspheme my King and my Savior?" The crowds called for Polycarp's death, and within minutes had built a pyre for their victim. When he was tied to the pyre and flames came up around him, Polycarp thanked God for the blessing of sharing "the cup of thine Anointed."

Since Jesus submitted to the Father's plan and became the sacrificial Lamb of God, thousands of Christians have been martyred rather than deny that sacrifice. Jesus said, *"And I, if I am lifted up from the earth, will draw all people to Myself"* (John 12:32). In this lesson we see the love and compassion of Jesus as He prayed in full submission to the Father's will. Rejected by those He came to save, He nevertheless laid down His life for all who accept Him as their Passover lamb, the final sacrifice for sin. When we see the depth of His love, we can understand why so many have followed in His steps.

I. THE PRAYER (JOHN 17)

In the Upper Room, Jesus had given His farewell address to His bewildered disciples. Now in the Garden, Jesus turned from the disciples to the Father and offered Himself as the sacrificial Lamb. At the same time, He assumed the role of High Priest

EXPLORING THE NEW TESTAMENT

making intercession for man before Almighty God. Jesus prayed first for Himself, then for His disciples, and last for all believers down through the ages.

A. Jesus prayed for Himself.

Jesus talked to the Father about two kinds of glory: the unlimited glory which He had before coming to earth and the limited glory received from earth. Only the Father, Son, and Holy Spirit have unlimited glory—manifested only in heaven. Jesus asked that the Father return this glory to Him. This is the glory which God said Moses could not see and live. But someday we will behold His glory.

There is a limited glory which believers share with Jesus Christ. Jesus said He had brought glory to the Father by finishing the work He came to do. We too bring glory to God by doing His work and bearing fruit. To serve Jesus Christ and to grow in Him is to give Him glory.

B. Jesus prayed for His disciples.

Jesus did not pray for the world, but for those whom the Father had given Him. As the disciples believed, obeyed, and participated in His work, glory came to Jesus. But He knew that when He returned to the Father, the disciples must remain in the world, fighting a continuing battle against Satan. Jesus prayed that they would be protected, that they would have unity, and that they would be made holy.

C. Jesus prayed for all believers.

When Jesus walked across the Kidron Valley on His way to the Garden of Gethsemane, you and I were on His mind. Jesus prayed for all who would come to know Him. He asked the Father to give believers unity—not only that we might have joy, but also that His mission might go forward in the world.

Jesus closed His prayer with the promise that He would continue to make God known to us so that the love of God might be in us.

What a joy to know that our High Priest prayed for us even when He was here in the flesh, and that He continues to intercede for us before the throne of God.

For what three groups did Jesus pray in His High Priestly Prayer?

List three things you learned about "glory" from Jesus' prayer.

_____

_____

_____

_____

_____

How did Jesus define "eternal life"?

_____

_____

_____

_____

II. THE REJECTION (JOHN 18:1-19:16)

On the slopes of the Mount of Olives is an area known as the Garden of Gethsemane. It was in this garden that Jesus was rejected and betrayed by one of His own.

The character of Jesus shone like a bright light in the midst of darkness on the night He was betrayed. At least three things are significant. (1) Jesus knew what was to take place, and He was in complete command. (2) Jesus did nothing to stop the chain of events which moved rapidly to bring Him to the cross. (3) And, even in this dark hour, He was more concerned about His disciples than about Himself.

The character of mankind was also revealed that night, and stands in sharp contrast to that of Jesus, the Son of God.

A. Forsaken by His disciples

Even among the disciples, those closest to Jesus, there was betrayal. Judas Iscariot chose to betray the Son of God for 30 pieces of silver, but Jesus must have been most disappointed in Peter. In the Upper Room, Peter had declared that he would lay down his life for Jesus. And, he had shown great courage when he drew his sword and took on the soldiers who came to arrest Jesus. But later in the courtyard of the high priest Peter denied Jesus three times. Where were the other disciples? Earlier Jesus had said they would leave Him alone. And they did.

B. Rejected by the Jews

All the religious groups of Judaism rejected Jesus as the Messiah—the Zealots, the Sadducees, the Pharisees. The Pharisees, along with some officials from the chief priests and a detachment of Temple soldiers, came to the Garden to take Jesus to be tried before the Sanhedrin, the highest Jewish court of the land. He was questioned, but this court had no authority to pronounce the death penalty. This authority rested in the Roman governor.

C. Tried before the Romans

The charge which the Jews brought against Jesus was blasphemy, but this charge would not stand up in a Roman court. Blasphemy was a religious matter. By resorting to a lie, the Jews charged Jesus with insurrection—declaring Himself to be a king. Pontius Pilate, who judged Jesus, struggled with his decision. He believed that Jesus was innocent, but he was concerned about keeping his position as governor of Palestine. He wanted to set Jesus free. But he didn't have the courage to do so. In the end he sided with the Jews. He saved his job.

Today the rejection of Jesus the Messiah, the Son of God, goes on. In weakness, even believers desert Him in the face of persecution. Because of pride and desire for power men choose to go their own way—to hold on to their own feeble lights. Most reject Him out of indifference. Or, they go along with the crowd. They see no need for a Savior.

What are some of the reasons people of Jesus' day rejected Him as their Messiah and King?

Why do you think people today reject Jesus?

III. THE LAMB (JOHN 19:17-42)

Crucifixion was a Roman custom handed down from the Persians. It was regarded as the most horrible of deaths. While the bodies of Jews had to be taken down before sunset and buried, others were left hanging for days until vultures destroyed the bodies.

John makes us aware that in every way Jesus, the Lamb of God, was fulfilling His Father's plan revealed in Scripture. Centuries before, the prophets foretold that as Jesus hung on the cross a sponge soaked in wine vinegar would be lifted to His lips, his legs would not be broken, a spear would pierce His side.

Joseph of Arimathea asked Pilate for the body of the Lord. Nicodemus brought spices to anoint the body and the two men placed it in a nearby tomb.

How great is the love of God for us, His people.

EXPLORING

What does the title "Lamb of God" mean to you?

_____

_____

_____

_____

_____

What are the characteristics of Jesus which are most evident to you as you view Him on the cross?

_____

_____

_____

_____

Which character do you most identify with in this lesson: Peter, the other disciples, the women at the cross, or Joseph of Arimathea? Why?

_____

_____

_____

_____

_____

EXPLORING

THE NEW TESTAMENT

_____

_____

_____

_____

_____

_____

_____

_____

_____

_____

_____

_____

_____

_____

_____

_____

_____

_____

_____

_____

_____

_____

_____

_____

_____

_____

_____

SEARCH AND DECIDE

1. Reread the High Priestly Prayer in John 17, then read what followed in Mark 14:32-42. Explain in your own words what you believe were the deepest concerns Jesus had at this hour.

_____

_____

_____

_____

_____

_____

_____

2. Read Isaiah 53 and make a list of those things which point to the Messiah that John tells us about in this lesson. Is there any doubt in your mind that Jesus is the promised Messiah?

_____

_____

_____

_____

_____

_____

_____

3. John recorded the glory of the Lamb of God in the book of Revelation. Read the following and record what you learn. Include your reaction to these words of God. Revelation 5:11-13; 7:14; 17:14; 19:9; 21:23.

_____

_____

_____

_____

_____

_____

_____

JESUS: THE RESURRECTED CHRIST

READING:
John 20-21

OBJECTIVES:
1. You will identify with the disciples as they move from lack of understanding to recognition of Jesus and His victory, from mourning to joy.
2. You will accept as your own the lesson and the commission Jesus gave Peter.

THEMES:

Obedience	Believe/Know	Discipleship
Shepherd	Light/Darkness	Life/Death
Numbers	Bread	

EXPLORING

THE NEW TESTAMENT

Eugene O'Neill's play, *The Long Day's Journey Into Night*, expresses the viewpoint found in many of his plays—that while life may begin in hope, it ends in disappointment and despair. The play, about O'Neill's family, tragically portrays his parents as typical of the common man who sees his dreams fall apart and his life settle into emptiness and futility. Man struggles to cling to some small ray of hope, the playwright says, while at the same time he is moving steadily along into the darkness of night.

But this is not the viewpoint of the Christian. It is the opposite. From the darkness of sin in the Garden of Eden, God has steadily led His people toward ever-increasing light. He led the Israelites out of the darkness of slavery and into the Promised Land. And He asked His people, *"Who walks in darkness and has no light? Let him trust in the name of the Lord and rely upon his God"* (Isaiah 50:10). Then Jesus came proclaiming, *"I am the light of the world. He who follows Me shall not walk in darkness, but have the light of life"* (John 8:12).

For believers, life is a journey out of darkness into light. We live in hope—not despair. And because Jesus defeated death and rose from the grave victorious, we have full assurance that we too shall live forevermore.

Let's go back to that day 2,000 years ago when life looked dark indeed to the group of grieving disciples. On Friday, Joseph of Arimathea and Nicodemus had laid the body of Jesus in the dark tomb just before sunset. Those who loved Jesus couldn't be comforted and didn't remember His words, *"You will be sorrowful, but your sorrow will be turned into joy"* (John 16:20). But joy did come when the disciples discovered that Jesus was alive. They shouted, *"We have seen the Lord!"* And down through the ages Christians have replied, *"He has risen indeed!"*

I. THE EMPTY TOMB (JOHN 20:1-9)

In telling us what happened on the first day of the week following Jesus' crucifixion and burial, John chose to relate the story of three witnesses to the resurrection: Mary Magdalene, Simon Peter, and John himself. John doesn't use his name, but says "*the other disciple, whom Jesus loved*" (John 20:2).

Mary Magdalene was the first to go to the tomb early in the morning, sometime between three and six o'clock. As she drew near the tomb, she looked up and saw that the stone had been rolled away from the entrance. Her grief and her desire to minister to the dead kept her from thinking that Jesus was alive. Not stopping to look inside the tomb, she ran to Peter's house to tell friends gathered there that someone had taken away the Lord's body.

John, younger than Peter, arrived at the tomb first. But he hesitated at the door and didn't go into the sepulchre. Then Peter arrived and bolted right in. John made the point not only that he was the first to reach the tomb, but also that he was the first to believe that Jesus was indeed risen from the dead. John accepted the evidence: the tomb was empty.

We aren't sure when Peter first believed that Jesus was alive. But one thing is certain. No one expected Jesus to rise from the dead. His followers believed that someday He would return and take them to be with Him, but they didn't expect to find an empty tomb that first Easter morning.

How did Mary Magdalene react when she saw the empty tomb?

_____

_____

_____

_____

_____

Compare Peter's reaction and John's reaction to finding the tomb empty.

_____

_____

_____

_____

II. THE JOYFUL REUNION (JOHN 20:10-31)

A. Jesus appeared to Mary Magdalene.

When Peter and John left, Mary stayed at the tomb weeping and grieving for her Lord. She couldn't bring herself to leave. Looking inside the tomb she saw two angels who asked why she was weeping. Her answer tells us that she didn't understand that Jesus had risen from the dead.

As Mary turned around, Jesus spoke to her. She thought He was the gardener. But when Jesus spoke her name, *"Mary!"* she knew Him. She wanted to hold Jesus close, to touch Him. But Jesus wanted her to understand the spiritual relationship which His resurrection had now made possible. He sent her with a message to the others: *"I am ascending to My Father and your Father, and to My God and your God"* (John 20:17). Jesus established a family relationship.

B. Jesus appeared to the disciples.

We can't be sure how many of the disciples believed Mary's words. John did. Peter probably did. But they were all aware that they would be accused of stealing the body of Jesus. Fearfully, they gathered together behind locked doors. It was there Jesus found them.

He came to the disciples to bless them, to commission them, and to empower them. First Jesus gave them His peace. And the disciples were overjoyed. Next, He said, *"As the Father has sent Me, I also send you"* (John 20:21). They were to go forth free of fear and make the redemptive work of Jesus known to men. Last, Jesus breathed new life on the disciples and said, *"Receive the Holy Spirit."* Their mission was to be accomplished in the power of the Holy Spirit.

Have you ever gone through a time of discouragement and fear, a time when your hopes were dashed to the ground? Many of us have, and have experienced the joy of encountering the risen Christ who pointed our lives in a new direction. This is what happened to the disciples.

C. Jesus dealt with Thomas' doubt.

Thomas, like many throughout history, refused to believe in Jesus because he could not touch Him physically. Thomas wasn't with the other disciples when Jesus first appeared to them, and he didn't believe their testimony. A week later Jesus appeared again to the disciples—and Thomas was there.

Jesus knew Thomas' doubting heart and had him touch His hands and His side. The time for doubting was past. Thomas must believe. And he did.

Jesus had now brought Mary Magdalene and all the disciples to an understanding of His resurrection. They knew He was alive. He was the risen Christ.

Why did the disciples have such a hard time believing that Jesus was alive?

Briefly record a time in your life when Jesus took away your fear and gave you peace.

III. THE RETURN TO FISHING (JOHN 21:1-14)

The argument that Jesus appeared only as a vision, a hallucination, or a spirit, is quickly laid to rest by this third appearance to a group of the disciples. Here Jesus is flesh and blood. He warmed His hands by a charcoal fire, cooked fish, and ate with His friends. And His body still bore the marks of the nails and the Roman spear.

Seven of the disciples were fishing about 100 yards from shore on the Sea of Tiberias (Galilee) when they saw Jesus. Jesus had specifically chosen His disciples to become fishers of men. He had given them a new vocation, a new mission. When Jesus called to them from shore and asked if they had caught any fish, their answer was, "No." But when they obeyed His command to throw their net on the *right* side of the boat, their net was filled with 153 large fish.

John was the first to recognize Jesus, but it was Peter who jumped into the water and swam to Him. When the others landed, Jesus fed His disciples fish and bread which He had prepared for them. Once again they were reminded that they were to be fishers of men, shepherds of sheep, and servants, that many might be brought into the Kingdom of God.

In what way do all eight themes in this lesson come together in the story of the disciples' return to fishing? (John 21:1-14)

IV. THE RETURN TO MINISTRY (JOHN 21:15-25)

Jesus not only taught and ministered to the disciples as a group, but He was also concerned about each one as an individual. This is true for us today as well. Jesus knows when we need His special instruction or correction. On the shore of

Galilee, Jesus asked Peter three times if he loved Him. Each time Peter affirmed his love for his Lord, and each time Jesus called him to shepherd His sheep—to take care of them and feed them.

Why was Peter singled out? Because in the courtyard of the high priest Peter had denied that he was a disciple of Jesus. Peter needed to be forgiven and restored to ministry and service.

If Peter thought it had been difficult to stand up for Jesus that night in the courtyard, he must have been shaken when Jesus told him that he would follow his Master to the cross. But Peter never again denied Jesus. In life and in death he glorified God.

Jesus' plan for John was different from that of the other disciples, and Peter questioned this. But the Lord let Peter know that this was not his concern. Rather, He said, *"You follow Me."* And that is our task: to obey and follow Jesus wherever He leads us.

List three things that we should learn from Peter's failure and restoration.

_____

_____

_____

_____

_____

What does Jesus' command to Peter, *"Follow me,"* mean to you personally?

_____

_____

_____

_____

_____

SEARCH AND DECIDE

1. Keep John 20-21 in mind as you read the following. Then, write a statement of what you believe about the resurrection of Jesus Christ and all who belong to Him. Job 19:25-26; Acts 4:33; I Cor. 15:12-20.

_____

_____

_____

_____

_____

_____

_____

2. Read Mark 8:38. What bearing do you think Jesus' words here had on His reinstatement of Peter in John 21:15-23? How does this affect your life?

_____

_____

_____

_____

_____

_____

_____

Appendix 1

THE WORLD
OF THE NEW TESTAMENT

For years travelers in Europe have enjoyed staying in homes advertised as "Bed and Breakfast" accommodations. Recently these have become popular in the United States. If you are a foreign visitor, staying overnight in a private home offers an opportunity to meet the people, learn about their daily lives, sample their food, and become acquainted with their customs.

If only we could go back in time, we might be invited to spend the night with Zechariah and Elizabeth, or Mary and Martha. In Nazareth, we might even find a "Bed and Breakfast" home open to us near Mary and Joseph. If this were possible, what might we learn about the Roman emperors and the Herods? About the Pharisees and the Sadducees, family life, education of the children, religions of the people?

We do know that the world was in great need of a Messiah. For centuries the Jews had waited, hoped and prayed that God would send the Messiah of whom Isaiah wrote:

> "Prepare the way of the Lord;
> Make straight in the desert a
> highway for our God."
> Isaiah 40:3

Even though the greatest event in the history of the world took place in the first century, life went on as usual. Kings held court, Jews argued the Law in the synagogues, women had babies, and slaves prepared perfumed baths for Roman ladies.

Let's take a brief look at the land of Palestine during the time period God chose to send His Son into the world.

I. POLITICAL LIFE IN THE ROMAN EMPIRE

A. The Emperors

Eleven emperors ruled over the Roman empire during New Testament times. Jesus was born during the reign of Caesar Augustus (27 B.C.-A.D. 14); His public ministry and death occurred during the reign of Tiberius (A.D. 14-37). The birth and beginning expansion of the church came during the reigns of Caligula (A.D. 37-41), Claudius (A.D. 41-54) and Nero (A.D. 54 -68). All these emperors were worshiped as gods, yet they allowed the Jews to worship Jehovah and live much as they pleased, provided they did not interfere with the Roman government. But the Caesars lived in Rome, and the rulers who enforced Roman laws which affected the daily lives of the people of Palestine were the Herods.

B. The Herods

The Herods ruled as kings over Palestine by appointment of the Roman emperors. They were descendants of the Edomites who had moved into Idumea in the southern part of Judea when the Jews were in Babylonian exile.

While the Herods acknowledged God, often gave generously to the Temple, and occasionally worshiped there, they were power hungry. They were guided by their desire to please the Roman emperors who, with a single command, could remove them from their thrones. This meant keeping the peace in Palestine regardless of the cost.

Herod the Great was on the throne when Caesar Augustus came to power, and was king when Jesus was born. He was a merciless murderer whose only contribution to Judaism was the rebuilding of the Temple—a project still incomplete at the time Jesus ministered there. When Herod died in 4 B.C., Palestine was divided among his three sons: Archelaus (4 B.C.-A.D. 6) ruled over Judea and Samaria; Philip (4 B.C.-A.D. 34) had the northeast corner of Palestine, east of the Jordan River; and Antipas (4 B.C.-A.D. 39) took Galilee and Perea.

When Caesar Augustus removed Archelaus in A.D. 6, he replaced him with a procurator and made Judea a Roman province. Pontius Pilate was procurator when Jesus was tried before him.

Herod Agrippa I reunited the three areas of Palestine and ruled over them from A.D. 37-44. He is the Herod who first ordered Peter imprisoned and the Apostle James executed. He was followed by his son, Herod Agrippa II, who ruled to the end of the century. Agrippa II was involved in the decision to send Paul to Rome for trial. He sided with the Romans during the revolution of A.D. 66, and stood with them during the destruction of the Temple in A.D. 70.

C. The High Priests

Accepted as spokesmen for God, the High Priests in the first century A.D. had great power and authority. They were the central control in Judaism. The High Priest presided over the Sanhedrin in Jerusalem, the Supreme Court of the Jews, and served as mediator and advisor to the Roman procurator.

D. The Political Parties

Zealots actively opposed the Romans while Herodians supported them. The Pharisees usually obeyed Roman laws because they believed that God had brought them under foreign rule as punishment for their sins. The wealthier Sadducees tried to stay on good terms with the Romans for business reasons.

E. The Sanhedrin

The Sanhedrin was the highest Jewish court in the land. At one time the Sadducees had dominated the court, but in the first century Pharisees replaced them. This court of 70 men had great power in Judea to judge both religious and political matters. Local councils from the synagogues took care of cases outside Judea, but cases could be appealed to the Jerusalem Sanhedrin.

II. SOCIAL LIFE IN PALESTINE

A. Classes of Society

About three million Jews lived in Palestine during New Testament times—some wealthy, some poor, many slaves. Families of the priesthood and of leading rabbis were the aristocracy. Some were wealthy landowners like Nicodemus and Joseph of Arimathea. But the poor had to work hard to make a living, and beggars were everywhere. Women were the property of men, but were free to go about the land—even without veils. Corruption in politics, fraud in business, and deceit in religion were all common in Roman times.

B. Family Life

As head of the family, the father ruled over the household. Both marriage and divorce were private affairs and no laws governed either; however, it was the custom by this time to have only one wife. It was important for a Jewish woman to be able to have children— particularly boys. If a woman became a widow, she was cared for by her husband's family, and in the early church she was put on a charity list at age 60.

C. Languages

Four languages were used in Palestine: Latin was the official language of the Romans; Greek was spoken by all educated people; Aramaic was the language of the people who lived in the northeastern part of Palestine; and Hebrew was the language of the learned rabbis and Jewish aristocracy. Jesus probably used all of these at one time or another.

D. Education

At six years of age, Jewish boys started to school and sat in a semicircle on the floor before their teacher. The Old Testament books we have today were the only texts for reading and writing. Much of the scripture was memorized, and most reading was done aloud. Very bright boys continued their education beyond age 15 with some of the great rabbis. Girls, trained in the household arts, were not given a formal education.

E. Business and Finance

Most Jewish boys followed the trade of their fathers. Some were farmers or shepherds, fishermen or carpenters, lawyers or physicians. Roman currency was sound, and bankers and moneychangers did a thriving business. Excellent roads and seaports fostered free trade throughout the Empire.

III. RELIGIOUS LIFE IN PALESTINE

A. The Jews

The two major sects of Judaism were the Pharisees and Sadducees. The Pharisees numbered only about 6,000 men in the first century, but they were the most influential group in Jewish society. While they accepted the Torah, the Prophets, and the Writings, they stressed the outer forms of worship to the neglect of the inner spirit. They overlaid the Law of Moses with strict interpretations of their own, and laid heavy burdens on the poor. Jesus called them the "righteous" who needed no physician. They believed in the existence of angels and spirits, in immortality of the soul, and in resurrection of the body.

The Sadducees were fewer in number than the Pharisees, but were more powerful politically because of their wealth and positions. They strongly supported the Roman government and the high priests. Sadducees accepted the written Torah, but considered the Prophets and the Writings to have less authority. Unlike the Pharisees, they did not believe in the existence of angels or spirits, immortality of the soul, or resurrection of the dead.

While the Sadducees were very involved in public life, a group called the Essenes withdrew from society and settled into monastic life. Scholars believe that the Qumran community which produced the Dead Sea Scrolls discovered in 1947 was their headquarters. This group considered themselves to be the faithful remnant of Israel. They believed that by isolating themselves they could keep the levitical laws and give more time to the study of Scripture. They thought the soul, but not the body, was immortal.

The Hellenists were another branch of Judaism. This group adopted the Greek culture and language while retaining the Jewish faith. They had their own synagogues, and often came into conflict with the strict Jews at the Temple in Jerusalem. Later, guarding the Christian faith against the Greek influences of the Hellenists became a serious problem.

Not all first century Jews were Pharisees, Sadducees, Essenes, or Hellenists. Some simply lived out their lives with a deep devotion to God, keeping the festivals and sacrifices, and obeying the scriptures as they understood them. Mary and Joseph were in this group we call pietists, a word denoting reverence, obedience, and godliness.

Other Jews of the first century had become so disillusioned by the legalism and snobbery of the Pharisees and

Sadducees that they ignored the religious ceremonies. They were despised by the priests and rabbis; Jesus saw them as *"sheep without a shepherd."*

B. The Romans

The Romans had a pantheon of gods. Jupiter and Juno were primary ones, but every village had gods of earth and sky. People were superstitious and many looked to astrology to guide their lives. Most educated Romans respected the gods but gave them very little thought. Greek thought had strongly influenced the Romans to trust in their own reasoning and their own strength.

Appendix 2

THE LIFE OF CHRIST IN THE FOUR GOSPELS

	Matthew	Mark	Luke	John
I. CHILDHOOD				
Genealogy	1:1-17		3:23-38	
Announcement of birth of Jesus	1:18-25		1:26-38	
Birth of Jesus	1:24-25		2:1-7	
Announcement by angels			2:8-14	
Shepherds' visit			2:15-20	
First temple visit			2:21-38	
Visit of Wise Men	2:1-12			
Escape to Egypt	2:13-18			
Home to Nazareth	2:19-23		2:39	
Childhood and second temple visit			2:40-52	
II. BEGINNING MINISTRY				
Jesus is baptized in Jordan River	3:13-17	1:9-11	3:21-23	1:29-34
Jesus is tempted	4:1-11	1:12-13	4:1-13	
Wedding at Cana				2:1-11
Cleansing of temple in Jerusalem				2:12-22
Jesus and Nicodemus				3:1-21
Jesus and John the Baptist				3:22-31
Departs to Galilee	4:12	1:14	4:14	4:1-4
Ministry to the Samaritan woman				4:5-42
III. GALILEAN MINISTRY				
Jesus heals a nobleman's son				4:43-54
Jesus is rejected in His town: Nazareth			4:16-30	
First disciples are called	4:18-22	1:16-20	5:1-11	1:35-51
Jesus heals demoniac on the Sabbath		1:21-28	4:32-37	
Jesus heals Peter's mother-in-law	8:14-17	1:29-34	4:38-41	

	Matthew	Mark	Luke	John
First Galilean preaching tour	4:23-25	1:35-39	4:42-44	
Jesus heals leper	8:1-4	1:40-45	5:12-16	
Jesus heals a paralytic	9:1-8	2:1-12	5:17-26	
Jesus calls Matthew	9:9-13	2:13-17	5:27-32	
Jesus appoints 12 disciples		3:13-19	6:12-16	
Jesus preaches the Sermon on Mount	5:1-7:29		6:20-49	
Jesus heals a servant	8:5-13		7:1-10	
Jesus raises a widow's son			7:11-17	
Jesus is anointed by a sinful woman			7:36-50	
Jesus is accused of blasphemy	12:22-37	3:20-30	11:14-23	
Jesus teaches on the family	12:46-50	3:31-35	8:19-21	
Jesus' parables of the kingdom	13:1-52	4:1-34	8:4-18	
Jesus calms the sea	8:23-27	4:35-41	8:22-25	
Jesus heals a demoniac	8:28-34	5:1-20	8:26-39	

Jesus raises Jarius'
   daughter and heals
   woman's bleeding
	9:18-26	5:21-43	8:40-56	

Disciples are sent out	9:35-11:1	6:6-13	9:1-6	
John is beheaded	14:1-12	6:14-29	9:7-9	
Jesus feeds 5,000	14:13-21	6:30-34	9:10-17	6:1-14
Jesus walks on water	14:22-33	6:45-52		6:15-21
Jesus speaks out in synagogue	15:1-20	7:1-23		
Jesus heals the Syro-Phoenician	15:21-28	7:24-30		
Jesus feeds 4,000	15:32-39	8:1-9		
Jesus calls His disciples to confess and commit	16:13-26	8:27-37	9:18-25	
The Transfiguration	17:1-13	9:2-13	9:28-36	
Jesus teaches disciples humility	18:1-35	9:33-50	9:46-62	

IV. JUDEAN AND PEREAN MINISTRY

	Matthew	Mark	Luke	John
Jesus attends Feast of Tabernacles				7:2, 11-52

	Matthew	Mark	Luke	John
Jesus ministers to adulterous woman				7:53-8:11
Pharisees argue with Jesus				8:12-59
Jesus heals a man born blind				9:1-41
Jesus: The Good Shepherd				10:1-21
Jesus visits Mary and Martha			10:38-42	
Jesus teaches The Lord's Prayer			11:1-13	
Jesus raises Lazarus				11:1-44

V. THE LAST JOURNEY TO JERUSALEM

	Matthew	Mark	Luke	John
Jesus in Samaria and Galilee			17:11-18:14	
Jesus teaches on divorce	19:1-12	10:1-12		
Jesus blesses children	19:13-15	10:13-16	18:15-17	
Jesus talks to rich ruler	19:16-30	10:17-31	18:18-30	
Jesus talks about His death	20:17-19	10:32-34	18:31-34	
Jesus heals blind Bartimaeus		10:46-52	18:35-43	
Jesus talks to Zacchaeus			19:1-10	
Jesus visits Mary and Martha				11:55-12:1

VI. THE LAST WEEK

	Matthew	Mark	Luke	John
SUNDAY Triumphal Entry	21:1-11	11:1-10	19:29-44	12:12-19
MONDAY Jesus curses the fig tree		21:18-19	11:12-14	
Jesus cleanses the temple	21:12-13	11:15-18	19:45-48	
TUESDAY Disciples see withered fig tree		21:19-22	11:20-26	
Jesus meets opposition	21:23-23:39	12:1-44	20:1-47	
Jesus teaches about the end times	24-25	13:1-37	21:5-36	
Jesus is anointed in Bethany	26:6-13	14:3-9		12:2-11
Jesus' betrayal is planned	26:14-16	14:10-11	22:1-6	

	Matthew	Mark	Luke	John
WEDNESDAY...				
THURSDAY				
Passover Meal: The Last Supper	26:17-29	14:12-25	22:7-30	
Jesus comforts the disciples				14-16
Jesus' High Priestly Prayer				17
In the Garden of Gethsemane	26:36-46	14:32-42	22:39-46	18:1
THURSDAY NIGHT AND FRIDAY				
Jesus is betrayed and arrested	26:47-56	14:43-52	22:47-53	18:2-12
Jesus is tried	26:57-27:26	14:53-15:15	22:54-23:25	18:13-19:16
Jesus is crucified	27:27-56	15:16-41	23:26-49	19:17-30
Jesus is buried	27:57-60	15:42-46	23:50-54	19:31-42

VII. RESURRECTION AND ASCENSION

	Matthew	Mark	Luke	John
The empty tomb	28:1-8	16:1-8	24:1-12	20:1-10
Mary Magdalene and other women	28:9-10	16:9-11		20:11-18
Two on road to Emmaus		16:12-13	24:13-35	
Jesus appears to the disciples		16:14	24:36-43	20:19-31
Jesus and disciples by Sea				21:1-25
Jesus ascends to the Father	28:16-20	16:19-20	24:44-53	

Appendix 3

NEW TESTAMENT SURVEY

4 Gospels and Acts

Matthew	Mark	Luke	John	Acts
A.D. 50–70 To: Jews	A.D. 50–70 To: Gentiles	A.D. 50–70 To: Gentiles	A.D. 85–90 To: Believers and Nonbelievers	A.D. 62–63 To: Theophilus

14 Letters of Paul

Romans	I Corinthians	II Corinthians	Galatians	Ephesians	Philippians	Colassians	I Thessalonians
A.D. 57 To: Believers at Rome	A.D. 55 To: Believers at Corinth	A.D. 55 To: Believers at Corinth	A.D. 53–57 To: Believers at Galatia	A.D. 60 To: Believers at Ephesus	A.D. 60 To: Believers at Philippi	A.D.60 To: Believers at Colossae	A.D. 51 To: Believers at Thessalonica

II Thessalonians	I Timothy	II Timothy	Titus	Philemon	Hebrews
A.D. 51 To: Believers at Thessalonica	A.D. 63 To: Timothy	A.D. 66–67 To: Timothy	A.D. 63–65 To: Titus	A.D. 60 To: Philemon	A.D. 68 To: Jewish Christians

7 More Letters, and Revelation

James	I Peter	II Peter	I John	II John	III John	Jude	Revelation
A.D. 45 or 60 To: Jewish Christians	A.D. 60–64 To: Jewish and Gentile Believers	A.D. 65–68 To: Christians in Asia Minor	A.D. 85–95 To: Believers	A.D. 85–95 To: The chosen lady and her children	A.D. 85–95 To: Gaius	A.D. 80 To: Believerss	A.D. 95 To: The Church

Appendix 4

ROMAN EMPERORS:
THE CAESARS

Augustus	27 B.C.-A.D. 14
Tiberius	A.D. 14-37
Caligula	A.D. 37-41
Claudius	A.D. 41-54
Nero	A.D. 54-68
Galba, Otho and Vitellius	A.D. 68-69
Vespasian	A.D. 69-79
Titus	A.D. 79-81
Domitian	A.D. 81-96

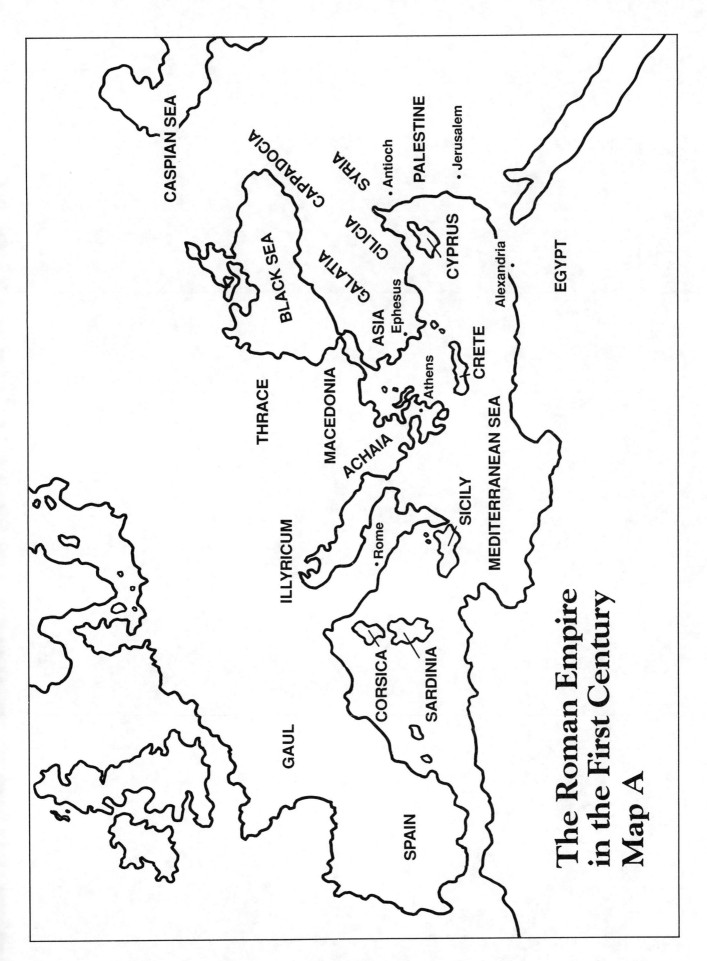

The Roman Empire
in the First Century
Map A

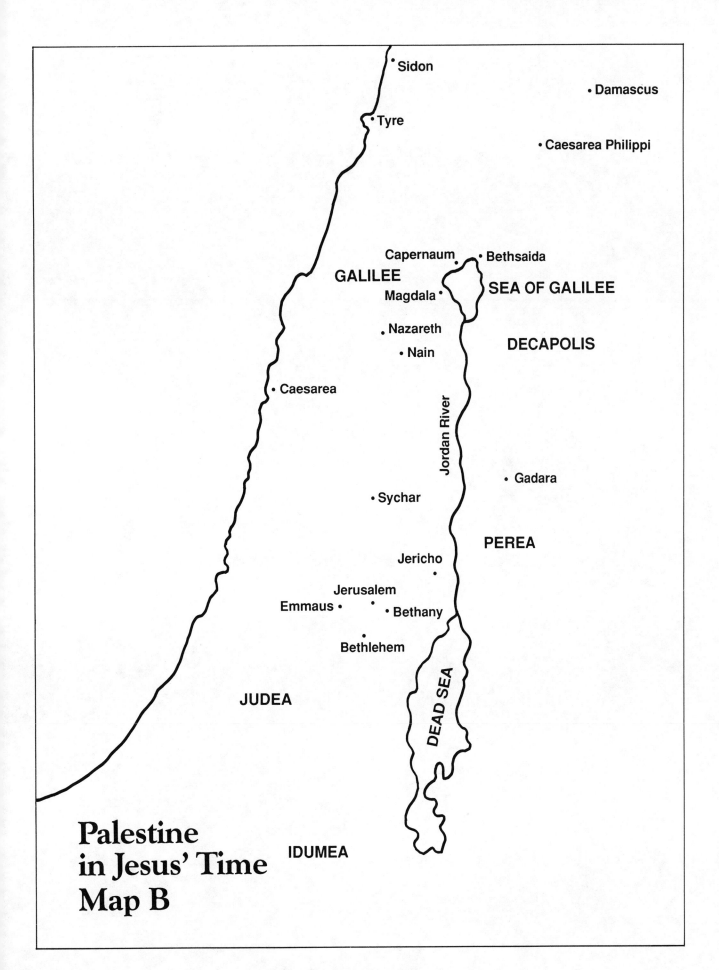

Sidon

• Damascus

• Tyre

• Caesarea Philippi

Capernaum • • Bethsaida

GALILEE

SEA OF GALILEE

Magdala •

DECAPOLIS

• Nazareth

• Nain

• Caesarea

Jordan River

• Gadara

• Sychar

PEREA

Jericho

Jerusalem

Emmaus • • • Bethany

Bethlehem

DEAD SEA

JUDEA

**Palestine
in Jesus' Time
Map B**

IDUMEA

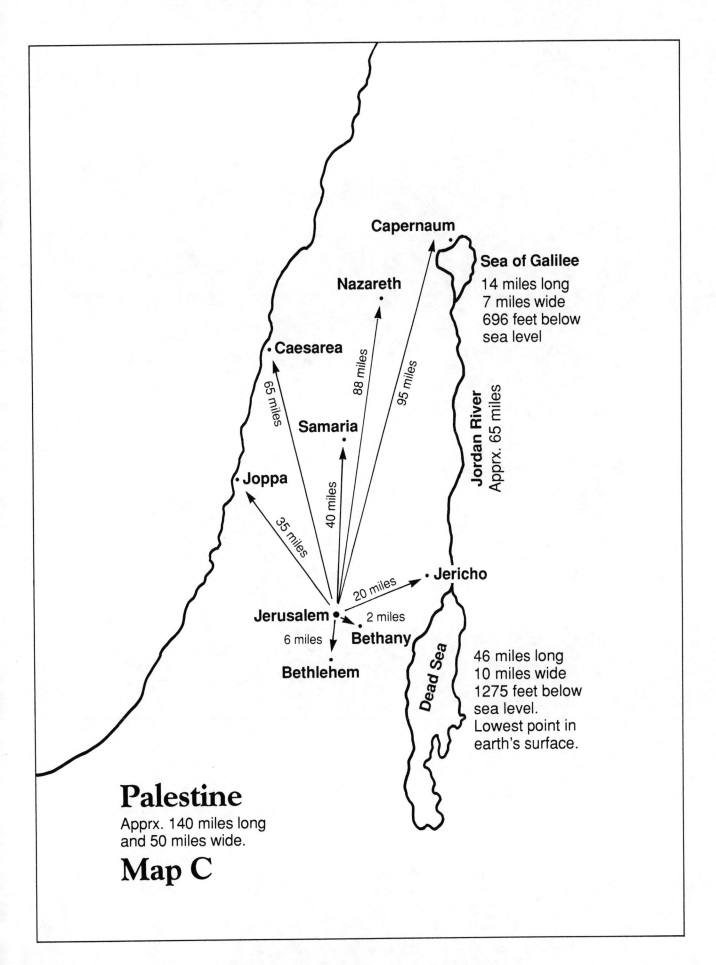

Capernaum

Sea of Galilee
14 miles long
7 miles wide
696 feet below
sea level

Nazareth

Caesarea

65 miles

88 miles

95 miles

Samaria

Jordan River
Apprx. 65 miles

Joppa

40 miles

35 miles

• **Jericho**

20 miles

Jerusalem •   • 2 miles

6 miles   **Bethany**

Bethlehem

Dead Sea

46 miles long
10 miles wide
1275 feet below
sea level.
Lowest point in
earth's surface.

Palestine

Apprx. 140 miles long
and 50 miles wide.

Map C

BIBLIOGRAPHY

Alon, Azaria. *The Natural History of the Land of the Bible*. Garden City, NY: Doubleday and Co., Inc., 1978.

Augsburger, Myron S. *Matthew*. Vol. 1 of *The Communicator's Commentary*. Ed. Lloyd J. Ogilvie. Waco, Texas: Word Books, 1982.

Austin, Bill R. *Austin's Topical History of Christianity*. Wheaton, IL: Tyndale House Pub., 1983.

Bruce, F.F., General Editor. *International Bible Commentary*. Rev. Ed. Grand Rapids: Zondervan, 1986.

_____. *Israel and the Nations*. Grand Rapids: Wm. B. Eerdmans Pub. Co., 1963.

_____. *The Hard Sayings of Jesus*. Downers Grove, IL: InterVarsity Press, 1983.

Blaiklock, Edward M., and R.K. Harrison, eds. *Dictionary of Biblical Archaeology*. Grand Rapids: Regency, 1983.

Buttrick, George Arthur, et al., eds. *The Interpreter's Bible*. 12 vols. Nashville, TN: Abingdon, 1953.

Carter, James E. *John*. Vol. 18 of *Layman's Bible Book Commentary*. Nashville, TN: Broadman Press, 1984.

Clarke, Adam. *Adam Clarke's Commentary on the Bible*. Abridged by Ralph Earle. Grand Rapids: Baker Book House, 1967.

Cole, Alan. *The Gospel According to St. Mark*. Vol. 2 of *Tyndale New Testament Commentaries*. Grand Rapids: Wm. B. Eerdmans Pub. Co., 1977.

Crapps, Robert W., Edgar V. McKnight and David A. Smith. *Introduction to the New Testament*. New York: The Ronald Press Co., 1969.

Crissey, Clair M. *Matthew*. Vol. 15 of *Layman's Bible Book Commentary*. Nashville, TN: Broadman Press, 1981.

Dean, Robert J. *Luke*. Vol. 17 of *Layman's Bible Book Commentary*. Nashville, TN: Broadman Press, 1983.

Douglas, J.D., ed. *Illustrated Bible Dictionary*. 3 vols. Wheaton, IL: Tyndale House Pub., 1981.

Earle, Ralph, A. Elwood Sanner and Charles L. Childers. *Matthew, Mark, Luke*. Vol. 6 of *Beacon Bible Commentary*. Kansas City, MO: Beacon Hill Press, 1964.

Edersheim, Alfred. *The Life and Times of Jesus the Messiah*. 2 vols. Grand Rapids: Wm. B. Eerdmans Pub. Co., 1969.

Foster, Dave, ed. *Jerusalem*. Paulton, Great Britain: Purnell and Sons, Ltd., 1980.

Fredrikson, Roger L. *John*. Vol. 4 of *The Communicator's Commentary*. Ed. Lloyd J. Ogilvie. Waco, Texas: Word Books, 1985.

Godwin, Johnnie C. *Mark*. Vol. 16 of *Layman's Bible Book Commentary*. Nashville, TN: Broadman Press, 1979.

Gower, Ralph. *The New Manners and Customs of Bible Times*. Chicago: Moody Press, 1987.

Gundry, Robert H. *A Survey of the New Testament*. Grand Rapids: Zondervan, 1970.

Guthrie, D., J.A. Motyer, et al. *New Bible Commentary*. Rev. Grand Rapids: Wm. B. Eerdmans Pub. Co., 1970.

Guthrie, Donald. *New Testament Introduction*. Downers Grove, IL: InterVarsity Press, 1974.

Harrison, Everett F. *Introduction to the New Testament*. Rev. Ed. Grand Rapids: Wm. B. Eerdmans Pub. Co., 1971.

Henry, Carl F.H., ed. *The Biblical Expositor*. Vol. 3. Grand Rapids: Baker Book
    House, 1960.

Henry, Matthew. *A Commentary on the Whole Bible*. Vol. 5. Old Tappan, N.J.:
    Fleming H. Revell Co., n.d.

Johnson, Paul. *Civilizations of the Holy Land*. London: Weidenfeld and Nicolson,
    1979.

Keller, Werner. *The Bible as History*. New York: Bantam, 1973.

Kenyon, Kathleen. *The Bible and Recent Archaeology*. Rev. Ed. by P.R.S. Moorey.
    Atlanta: John Knox Press, 1987.

Larson, Bruce. *Luke*. Vol. 3 of *The Communicator's Commentary*. Ed. Lloyd J.
    Ogilvie. Waco, Texas: Word Books, 1983.

Mayfield, Joseph H. and Ralph Earle. *John-Acts*. Vol. 7 of *Beacon Bible
    Commentary*. Kansas City, MO: Beacon Press, 1965.

McKenna, David L. *Mark*. Vol. 2 of *The Communicator's Commentary*. Ed. Lloyd J.
    Ogilvie. Waco, Texas: Word Books, 1982.

Morris, Leon. *The Gospel According to St. Luke*. Vol. 3 of *Tyndale New Testament
    Commentaries*. Grand Rapids: Wm. B. Eerdmans Pub. Co., 1982.

Myers, Allen C. *The Eerdmans Bible Dictionary*. Rev. Ed. Grand Rapids: Wm. B.
    Eerdmans Pub. Co., 1987.

Paschall, H. Franklin and Herschel H. Hobbs, eds. *The Teacher's Bible
    Commentary*. Nashville, TN: Broadman Press, 1972.

Pfeiffer, Charles F. and Everett F. Harrison, eds. *The Wycliffe Bible Commentary*.
    Chicago: Moody Press, 1962.

Ryken, Leland. *The Literature of the Bible*. Grand Rapids: Zondervan, 1974.

Tasher, R.V.G. *The Gospel According to St. Matthew*. Vol. I of *Tyndale New
    Testament Commentaries*. Grand Rapids: Wm. B. Eerdmans Pub. Co., 1983.

_____. *The Gospel According to St. John*. Vol. 4 of *Tyndale New Testament
    Commentaries*. Grand Rapids: Wm. B. Eerdmans Pub. Co., 1981.

Tenny, Merrill C., Steven Barabas, et al., eds. *The Zondervan Pictorial Encyclopedia
    of the Bible*. 5 vols. Grand Rapids: Zondervan, 1975-76.

Tenny, Merrill C. *New Testament Survey*. Grand Rapids: Wm. B. Eerdmans Pub.
    Co., 1961.

Thompson, Leonard L. *Introducing Biblical Literature*. Englewood Cliffs, NJ:
    Prentice-Hall, Inc., 1978.

Wilson, Walter Lewis. *Wilson's Dictionary of Bible Types*. Grand Rapids: Wm. B.
    Eerdmans Pub. Co., 1957.

Wright, G. Ernest, et al., eds. *Great People of the Bible and How They Lived*.
    Pleasantville, N.Y.: Reader's Digest Assn., Inc., 1979.